Scholastic World Cultures

TROPICAL AND SOUTHERN AFRICA

by Allen R. Boyd
and John Nickerson

FOURTH EDITION

Consultant

LEONARD THOMPSON
Professor of History
Yale University

Readability Consultant

LAWRENCE B. CHARRY, Ed.D.

📖 SCHOLASTIC INC.

Titles in This Series
CANADA
CHINA
GREAT BRITAIN
THE INDIAN SUBCONTINENT
JAPAN
LATIN AMERICA
MEXICO
THE MIDDLE EAST
SOUTHEAST ASIA
THE SOVIET UNION AND EASTERN EUROPE
TROPICAL AND SOUTHERN AFRICA
WESTERN EUROPE

ISBN 0-590-34633-4

12 11 10 9 8 7 6   1 2 3 4 5/9
                                                               23

Allen R. Boyd, author of the vignettes of African life in Chapters 3,6,7,9,11,and 13, is a former editor of Scholastic Book Services who worked two years as advisor to the Information and Education Service of the Zaire National Army and has traveled extensively in Africa. He is director/founder of a firm that distributes African books, documents, and microfilms to research centers throughout the world.

General Editor for WORLD CULTURES: Carolyn Jackson
Associate Editor: LeRoy Hayman
Assistant Editor: Elise Bauman
Contributing Author: John Nickerson
Special Editor: Maura Christopher
Teaching Guide Editor: Frances Plotkin

Art Director and Designer: Irmgard Lochner
Art Assistant: Wilhelmina Reyinga
Photo Editor: Elnora Bode

Cover: Two young Ethiopian villagers near the city of Harar.

TROPICAL
AND SOUTHERN
AFRICA

Table of Contents

AFRICA

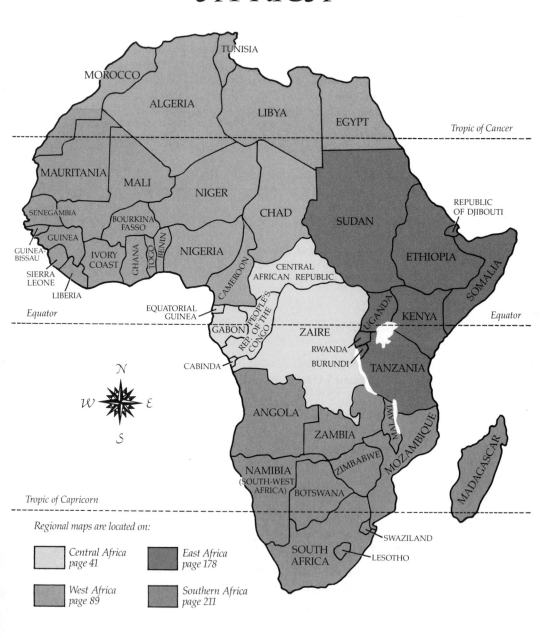

TUNISIA

MOROCCO

ALGERIA

LIBYA

EGYPT

Tropic of Cancer

MAURITANIA

MALI

NIGER

CHAD

SUDAN

REPUBLIC
OF DJIBOUTI

SENEGAMBIA

BOURKINA
FASSO

GUINEA

GUINEA-
BISSAU

IVORY
COAST

GHANA

TOGO

BENIN

NIGERIA

CENTRAL
AFRICAN REPUBLIC

ETHIOPIA

SOMALIA

SIERRA
LEONE

LIBERIA

CAMEROON

Equator

EQUATORIAL
GUINEA

GABON

REP. OF THE
PEOPLES
CONGO

ZAIRE

UGANDA

KENYA

Equator

CABINDA

RWANDA

BURUNDI

TANZANIA

ANGOLA

ZAMBIA

MALAWI

MOZAMBIQUE

MADAGASCAR

ZIMBABWE

NAMIBIA
(SOUTH-WEST
AFRICA)

BOTSWANA

Tropic of Capricorn

SWAZILAND

SOUTH
AFRICA

LESOTHO

N
W *E*
S

*I was asleep,
I woke – someone calls me:
"You're asleep, Mugala!
Come out here and see
How the ground is ringing!"*

—SUMBWA POEM (TANZANIA)

PROLOGUE

FROM
THE
INSIDE OUT

A SMILING, well-scrubbed black girl waves her hand at the teacher in a neat but simple classroom. A broad-shouldered African in goggles and coveralls works carefully with his complicated machinery. Herds of wild elephants make their way through broad, open valleys. African villagers do their "tribal dance" in a forest clearing.

This is Africa — or at least the way it's portrayed in many of today's books about the continent.

These books influence the way non-Africans view the world's least understood continent. Most of the books are attempts to explain what non-Africans think is important about Africa. That is, they look at the continent from the outside in.

This book takes a slightly different approach. It does not concern itself mainly with what outsiders think is important in Africa. Instead, it attempts to describe what is important to most Africans. In other words, it tries to look at Africa from the inside out.

More than 450 million people live in Africa. Most gain their living from the soil. Eight out of 10 Africans still live in the small villages of the vast interior and feel little or no real loyalty to their central governments. Most are unable to read or write.

What is important to these people? Family, friends, religion, self-respect, health, wealth — these all mean as much to Africans as they do to Americans. But some of these words mean one thing to Africans and another to Americans.

Africa is more than three times as large as the United States. It is far too large to be described in great detail in any one book. This book does not deal with Africans living north of the Sahara in the countries which border the Mediterranean Sea. These people are mostly Arabs and Berbers and are discussed in *The Middle East,* another book in the Scholastic WORLD CULTURES series.

In the following pages we will be concerned only with those nations wholly or partly south of the Sahara — the area known as Tropical and Southern Africa. The book includes a story about a London-trained lawyer who's on the top rung of the social ladder in Ghana.* It also includes a story about Pygmies,* whose traditional way of life is still largely unchanged. But most of the stories are about Africans who might be considered more typical of the continent's people as a whole. Here is Africa "from the inside out."

---

*See Pronunciation Guide.

1
CONTINENT
OF
ISOLATION

Chapter 1

The Land

How do you make a movie about Africa?

One way *not* to do it was the way it was done by one American camera crew in the years before World War II. At the time, Hollywood had just "discovered" the continent, and the producers sent a camera crew to do some filming on location. The team went to a spot near the Equator in Kenya,* took its pictures, then sent the rushes home.

The spot looked likely enough on a map. But back in Hollywood, the producers were startled to find that the film showed only desert and scrubland. "Where's all the jungle?" the movie executives fumed. And so the camera crew had to travel a thousand miles from their original location to find a jungle that Hollywood considered "typically African."

The mix-up shows how incorrect some American attitudes are toward Africa. Like the Hollywood producers, many of us have fairly fuzzy notions of what is "typically African." Often enough, we have picked up these notions at our local movie theaters, watching Tarzan as he swings from a jungle tree or slogs through some soupy swamp. Such films have prompted us to mistake the Africa of a Hollywood studio for the Africa which really exists.

Actually, the real Africa is a lot more exciting than the Africa of our imaginings. As the world's second largest continent, Africa is far larger, far wider, and far more varied than anything that can be caught on a movie screen. Africa occupies a fifth of the earth's total land surface. Within its shores lie the world's longest river (the Nile), the world's largest desert (the Sahara), and some of the most spectacular scenery to be found anywhere.

If that's the case, what is the "real" Africa really like? Let's look at a few of the current fictions about the African landscape and the facts which contradict them:

Fiction: Since Africa straddles the Equator, most of the continent is made up of jungle similar to that along the Amazon River in Brazil.

Fact: True, a lengthy strip of central Africa does sit astride the Equator. But surprisingly little of this land is rain forest. Only about one seventh of the continent's surface is such a forest. Both Asia and South America have larger rain forests than Africa has.

Most of Africa's jungle lies in two main areas. One is the Zaïre* River Basin (formerly the Congo Basin) in the center of the continent — an area drenched by up to 90 inches of rainfall every year. The other area is the coast of West Africa along the Gulf of Guinea.* Here the rain forest covers only the

14

✑ The "Africa" of a Hollywood
movie studio is often
a far cry from the Africa
which really exists.

---

narrow lip of the continent, in places reaching inland
no more than 150 miles.

᛫ What African rain forests lack in size they make up
for in vegetation. Here some trees grow so tall that
the lowest branches are some 60 feet off the ground.
The foliage grows thickest along riverbanks, where
enormous ferns, creepers, and evergreens vie for
water and air.

Elsewhere in Africa, however, forests are not plen-
tiful, and in some spots it's hard to find a single tree.
Three quarters of the continent is made up of grasslands, which vary in appearance from place to place.
The grasslands closest to the Equator are dotted with
woods and thickets. Other grasslands are as dry and
open as the cattle country of the American South-
west. Though these grasslands differ, none of them
is like the dank, dark jungle of the Tarzan epics.

Fiction: Like the other continents of the world, Africa is made up mostly of lowlands.

Fact: It's certainly true that the world's other continents are made up mostly of lowlands. Only about
half of Europe, for example, manages to rise 500 feet
above sea level. But in Africa 90 percent of the land
is more than 500 feet high. In large areas of eastern
Africa, the average elevation reaches a whopping
5,000 to 6,000 feet or more — about a mile above
sea level.

Basically, Africa is an enormous plateau which
slopes upward from west to east. But the African plateau isn't all one smooth tableland. On the contrary,

15

❧ Basically, Africa is an enormous, lumpy plateau which slopes upward from west to east.

Caught between sky and sea, the central highlands of Ethiopia march down the eastern edge of Africa in lonely grandeur. Are highlands land features you usually think of as "African"?

it's very bumpy and lumpy. Included in the plateau are five major river basins, a number of mountains, and one of the longest valleys in the world — the Great Rift Valley, which snakes through eastern Africa from Mozambique* in the south all the way to the Red Sea in the north.

But a dominant feature of the continent is its high altitude. In the northeast, in Ethiopia,* the highlands rise to a cloud-rubbing altitude of 14,000 feet. Farther south, the peaks of Mount Kilimanjaro* and Mount Kenya soar several thousand feet higher. Though Mount Kenya sits smack on the Equator, it remains snowcapped all year long.

Fiction: Throughout most of Africa, the heat is sweltering, and rainfall is heavy the year round.

Fact: Sure, Africa has its hothouse regions where temperatures often shoot above 100 degrees Fahrenheit. But such areas are more of an exception than a rule. In the northernmost and southernmost parts of the continent, for example, sea breezes bring mild weather throughout the year. Along the Equator in Kenya, highland winds often cool the air to a bitter chill.

Not even in the rain forests do temperatures normally get too far out of hand. In these areas clouds blot out the sun's rays for most of every day. Still, there's no denying that jungle weather has a tropical touch. It does get sticky, and the usual problem is, as the saying goes, not the heat but the humidity.

For the most part, African rain forests are as damp as their name suggests. Some areas receive as much as 300 inches of rain a year. Outside of these forests, however, Africa is not the rainswept continent it's often cracked up to be. Over large areas of the continent, it's just the opposite — an arid, parched land where rain rarely falls at all.

Throughout most of the continent, Africans divide their year into wet and dry seasons. Even so, they dare not take the rain too much for granted. Months that are supposed to be wet sometimes turn out to be dry. When such droughts occur, crops are damaged and famine can result.

So Africa is a good deal higher and somewhat drier than many of us have imagined. Most of it would be a bit too nippy for a bare-chested Tarzan clad only in animal skins. On the slopes of Mt. Kilimanjaro, Tarzan would find it hard to avoid frostbite. But in the Sahara in the northern part of Africa, or in the Kalahari* Desert in the southern part, he would risk a severe case of sunburn.

Why, then, have we accepted Tarzan's Africa as fact for so long? Why have Europeans and Americans held so many mistaken notions of African geography?

One reason for such ignorance is the continent's isolation. This isolation, in turn, stems largely from the geography of Africa itself. Nature has given the continent few easy entryways. As a result, outsiders curious enough to go exploring have found Africa a mammoth obstacle course.

Obstacle number one has been the age-old problem of reaching the continent by sea. One close look at a map will tell you why so few sailors over the centuries chose to make the trip. Though Africa is the world's second largest land mass, it has one of the world's straightest coastlines. Thus, it has few natural harbors where sailors feel safe in anchoring their ships.

Weather conditions along parts of the coast further discourage sea voyages. At the northwestern bulge of Africa, for example, winds and currents both push southward, making it difficult for sailors to head north. At the southern tip of the continent, around the Cape of Good Hope, a warm current from the eastern coast collides with a colder one from the west, sometimes creating furious storms.

Obstacle number two is to be found along the continent's waterways. None of Africa's major rivers is navigable for its entire length. Where they descend from the highlands of the interior to the coastal lowlands, most rivers tumble into rapids and waterfalls. The danger to travelers is obvious. Instead of cruising down these rivers, unwary mariners may easily end up swimming in them.

By now you may have already identified obstacle number three: the difficulty of reaching into the continent by land. Some land routes have been traveled for centuries — by way of the western rim of Asia and the Mediterranean countries in the north. But all of these routes meander across the empty wastes of the Sahara. These routes have long been followed by merchants with camel caravans. But the Sahara's heat and lack of water do not welcome more casual visitors.

Africa, then, is a land of barriers, barriers, and still more barriers. Deterred by its obstacles for centuries, most would-be travelers have done their exploring on other continents. Rarely has Africa been well understood by outsiders. All too often it has been dismissed as the "dark continent," filled with mysteries beyond imagination.

Nowadays, however, all that is being changed. More and more modern highways are stitching African cities together. More and more airlines are linking these cities with the rest of the world. As more and more travelers crisscross the continent, more and more misunderstandings come tumbling down. And the dark continent begins to seem — well — much brighter than we thought.

Double-check

Review

1. How much of the earth's land surface does Africa occupy?

2. What is the name of the world's longest river? The largest desert?

3. How much of Africa's surface is rain forest?

4. How much of Africa's land is more than 500 feet high?

5. Why are there few natural harbors in Africa?

Discussion

1. In the past, Hollywood movie producers helped to create an image of Africa that was quite different from the real Africa. How does the Africa shown in today's films and television shows compare with the continent as described in this chapter?

2. How do Africa's land characteristics differ from those of North America? How are they similar? Give examples to support your answers.

3. What are some questions about Africa that you would like to have answered by your study of this book?

Activities

1. A committee of students might be formed to prepare a large wall map of Africa for use with this and future chapters. They could use the map on page 6 as a guide, and then add information to it from other maps, including maps in this book.

2. Two words in the Prologue and seven words in Chapter 1 are starred (*). This indicates that these words are in the Pronunciation Guide at the back of the book. A committee of students might assume primary responsibility for teaching fellow students how to pronounce these words. They could do this, in advance, for all future chapters.

3. The photo essays near the center of this book contain several photos showing the diversity of land in Africa. You might look at these photos now, and then mark on a map the places they show.

Skills

SIX MAJOR DESERTS OF THE WORLD

Desert	Continent	Area (square miles)
Sahara	Africa	3,320,000
Gobi	Asia	500,000
Rub al-Khali	Asia	250,000
Great Victorian	Australia	250,000
Gibson	Australia	250,000
Kalahari	Africa	225,000

Source: *The 1980 World Almanac*

Use the table above and information in Chapter 1 to answer the following questions.

1. How many continents are listed in the table above?
(a) two (b) three (c) four

2. Which of the deserts listed above is the smallest?
(a) Gobi (b) Gibson (c) Kalahari

3. On which continent is the largest desert of those listed above?
(a) Africa (b) Asia (c) North America

4. Which desert listed above is larger than the other five deserts combined?
(a) Rub al-Khali (b) Sahara (c) none

5. How many square miles are covered by the major desert in southern Africa?
(a) 3,320,000 (b) 225,000 (c) 250,000

Chapter 2

Patterns of Settlement

ABOUT THE SAFEST WAY to sum up the African people is to say that it's difficult to sum them up in a simple phrase or two. Pick a statement — almost any statement — and, if it concerns Africans, it's likely to be qualified by a series of "ifs," "ands," or "buts."

Consider something as simple as the population of the continent, for example. Experts tell us that Africa now has a total population of more than 450 million, *but* . . . The reason for the "but" is that these experts don't exactly know how many people now live on the continent — not even to the nearest few thousand. Poor roads hinder census takers in some areas, and

In the northern Nigerian city of Kano, Arab influence is strong, as the flowing lines of the buildings demonstrate.

distrust on the part of local residents hinders them in others. As a result, many of Africa's population figures can be taken as only rough estimates.

For the sake of argument, however, let's say that the 450-million figure is more or less right. Now let's examine it further. With all those millions, Africa should be a fairly heavily settled continent. Well, in some ways it is, and in other ways it isn't.

How so? To begin with, Africa occupies one fifth of the earth's entire land surface. Yet its people make up only one tenth of the world's population. Compare the two fractions, and you'll see that the African continent is not nearly as congested as some other areas of the world. By contrast with, say, the Indian subcontinent, Africa is actually fairly roomy.

But . . . even that statement needs to be qualified a bit. The fact is that some parts of Africa are overcrowded, while others — the driest regions — are scarcely inhabited at all. In the marshy coastal lands of southern Nigeria,* for example, overpopulation is a problem. Congestion also besets the highland lakes area of eastern Africa (including parts of Uganda,* Kenya, Rwanda,* and Burundi*).

The reasons for such congestion go back to the land itself. Like people everywhere, Africans tend to live in places where nature is kindest. Since the majority of Africans are farmers, they have sought out areas of fertile soil and dependable rain. Then they have flocked to these areas in large numbers.

Such a buildup of people suggests the eventual growth of cities, and in some parts of Africa cities are growing by leaps and bounds. But these cities have not overtaken rural areas in importance — not yet, anyway. Only two out of every 10 Africans live in a city of 20,000 or more people. The vast majority live in small villages. And even many city-dwellers main-

POPULATION DISTRIBUTION

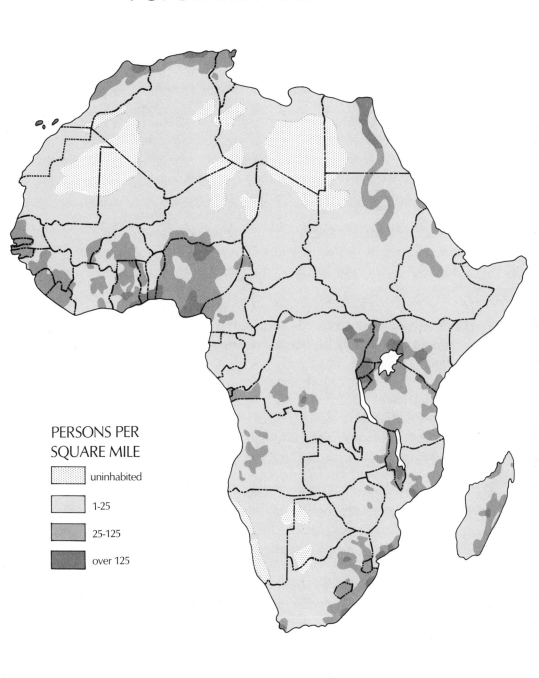

PERSONS PER
SQUARE MILE

uninhabited

1-25

25-125

over 125

tain close ties to the villages where they were born (see page 167).

African villages vary widely in appearance from one location to another. They may consist of leaf-covered huts in a forest clearing or thatched houses on an open plain. They may lie along highways or railroad lines or stand alone in the wilderness. And they differ just as widely in their customs and traditions. All this makes it impossible to describe the African people in a single, sweeping phrase.

The job gets even trickier when it becomes a matter of identifying who these people are.

Scholars with a fondness for sorting people into categories have sorted and resorted the African people in a number of different ways. They have classified Africans according to the countries they live in, the languages they speak, and the ethnic ties they hold dear. We will be taking a closer look at all three of these "identification tags" later in this book. But for the moment let's start with one of the broadest tags of all — that of physical features.

It is an obvious fact that people differ in physical features such as the color of their hair and the color of their skins. About nine out of 10 Africans have one or more of the following characteristics: dark skin, fairly flat noses, woolly hair, and thick lips. But that does not mean that all of these people have all of these characteristics — or even most of them. In many parts of Africa, for example, some so-called "black" Africans are quite light-skinned.

Nor is it enough to call attention to African physical features and let it go at that. Some traditional African ethnic groups are so distinct that they deserve special mention. Here are three ethnic groups which do:

*San.** Nearly all of Africa's approximately 100,000

LAND USE

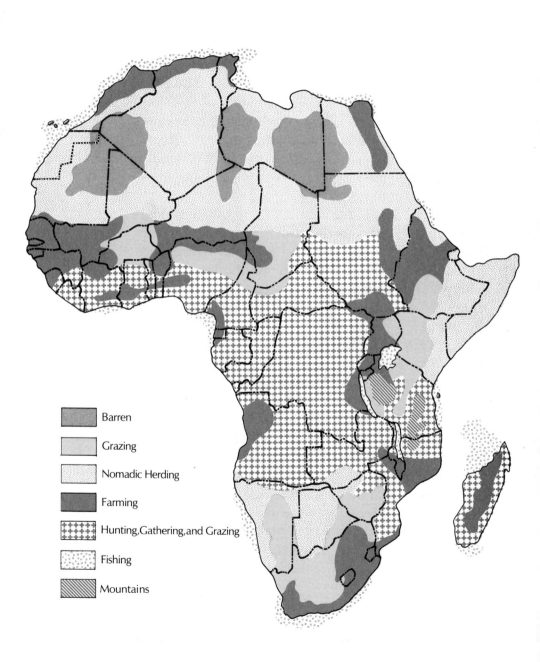

Barren

Grazing

Nomadic Herding

Farming

Hunting, Gathering, and Grazing

Fishing

Mountains

✎§ Like people everywhere, Africans tend to live in places where nature is kindest.

San, or Bushmen, make their home in the southern part of the continent. Many are desert-dwellers who go out hunting for their food. Short, with yellowish, wrinkled skin, true San people bear little resemblance to their neighbors. But in recent years many have been marrying with members of other groups. When they do, their children often have physical features of both groups.

Pygmies. Most of the continent's 50,000 or so Pygmies live as hunters in the Ituri* Forest of the Zaïre River Basin (see page 93). In a region where trees grow to giant size, the Pygmies simply don't. On the average, they stand no taller than four feet, nine inches. That makes them some of the tiniest people in the world.

Malgache. The Malgache — nearly seven million in number — are the people who live on Madagascar,* the island-nation off Africa's southeastern coast. Some of their ancestors migrated there from Southeast Asia in the dim past. On this rocky island, these Asians proceeded to mix with Arab and African peoples who also had migrated to their shores. As a result of all this mixing, the modern Malgache have physical features which blend several different strains.

Here, then, are only three of the many groups which have long called Africa home. In recent centuries, other groups have joined them. These newer settlers have arrived from several corners of the world.

Although African cities are growing at a rapid rate, eight out of 10 Africans still live in traditional villages such as this one in Ghana.

Listed by their place of origin, they are:

Europeans. There are more than four million Europeans in Africa today. Most have settled in eastern and southern Africa (see page 191).

Arabs. Perhaps as many as a million of them are widely scattered in the areas just south of the Sahara and in eastern Africa. The first Arabs to arrive in these areas came as early as 700 A.D. Most were merchants, sailing down the East African coast in search of trade. They stayed to build two important trading posts — Mombasa* and Dar es Salaam* — and to spread their religion, Islam* (see page 160). In recent years, many Arabs have come from Lebanon and Syria to eastern Africa, where they have played leading roles in business and commerce.

Indians. About one million Indians have settled, for the most part, in the cities of eastern and southern Africa. Most are descendants of men and women who came at the turn of this century from what is today India and Pakistan. Some of these settlers came to set up shops in East Africa's cities. Others came to construct a railroad from the East African coast to Uganda. Still others came to work in the sugar fields of Natal* in South Africa. Many drifted into commerce, some of them becoming quite well-to-do. They usually maintain tight bonds within their own community and do not associate much with outsiders. As a result, they are often resented by their black African neighbors. In a few cases, East African governments have even asked some Indians to leave.

These groups have not only swelled the number of people of Africa; they have also altered the pattern of African settlement, as we shall see. They have made Africans a varied and complex people. And, incidentally, they have made their region all the harder to describe in a simple, pat phrase.

*Dr. Louis Leakey and Mary Nichol Leakey
painstakingly digging and sorting earth in
Olduvai Gorge, Tanzania.*

SHAKING
THE
HUMAN FAMILY TREE

OF ALL THE MANY MYSTERIES probed by modern science, few are more baffling than the mystery of the human family tree. Experts have been studying the origins of the human race for many years, yet a number of perplexing questions remain:

About how many thousands or millions of years ago did that curious thing known as a human being first emerge on this planet?

Where did this emergence first take place?

What did modern humans emerge *from*?

Interestingly enough, scientists who lived in the early years of this century "knew" the answers to these puzzlers — or thought they did. They "knew" that modern humans first developed some 500,000 years ago, give or take a few thousand years. They "knew" that the birthplace of the human race was in central Asia. And they "knew" that humans evolved directly from apes.

All this "knowledge" once seemed certain — too certain, as it turned out. For in recent years new evidence has come forth to throw doubt on all three conclusions. Many scientists now believe that the first human being may have emerged as long ago as two million years. They also believe that this emergence took place in Africa rather than in Asia. And they think that humans evolved from a number of humanlike ancestors and not directly from the apes.

What's happened to change so many ideas? Mainly a startling set of breakthroughs in archaeology, the science which studies the remains of past human life. Much of the breaking through has taken place on the yellowing plains of East Africa. And much of it resulted from the shrewd detective work of a husband-wife team of fossil finders, Dr. Louis Leakey,* who died in 1972, and Mary Nicol Leakey.

Dr. Leakey was born in Kenya in 1903, the son of British missionaries. After finishing school in Britain, he returned to East Africa to do his fossil hunting. Mary Nicol had studied geology at the University of London and learned to scrape the walls of caves and dig for fossils before marrying Louis Leakey in 1936. For nearly half a century, they searched for missing clues to the human past.

In 1948 Dr. Leakey made his first major discovery. On an island in Lake Victoria in Kenya, he found the skull of an ape some 25 to 40 million years old. Upon close investigation, many scientists concluded that this creature could have been an ancestor of both man and apes. Their conclusion jarred the old notion that humans had descended directly from the apes. It also gave support to the idea that the human race first emerged in Africa.

That might have been discovery enough for most sleuths, but not for the Leakeys. They now traveled to other parts of the region to find out more. Their travels often took them to a 25-mile-long ravine called Olduvai* Gorge in what is now Tanzania.* What made Olduvai Gorge a likely spot for fossil hunting was the way the ravine had been formed.

Ages ago a river had cut through the gorge, carving out layer on layer of rock. As it worked its way through this rock, it had laid bare many different periods of the earth's life. The oldest period lay at the bottom of the gorge and the youngest at the top. Embedded in the rock along the sides of the ravine were the fossil remains of millions of years of world history.

The biggest find at Olduvai Gorge took place one hot July day in 1959. It was made by Mary Leakey who had gone out alone because her husband was ill. Toward the end of the day she spied a hunk of bone in the side of a rock deposit. The bone was a fragment of an ancient palate (roof of the mouth), and with it were some upper teeth. Both seemed humanlike. Excited, Mrs. Leakey raced off to get her husband, and the two returned to take a closer look.

The teeth and the palate were only the beginning of a monumental discovery. In time the Leakeys came upon some 400 bone fragments which they arranged to form a nearly complete skull. Dr. Leakey named the skull after the ancient East African land of Zinj.* As is the practice, he added a Latin ending to the name, making it a tongue twister: Zinjanthropus.* The skull was also nicknamed the "nutcracker" because of its enormous teeth.

Two aspects of the discovery were especially startling: One was the age of the skull, estimated by scientists to be almost two million years old. The other was the discovery of ancient stone tools, called "pebble tools," near the site where the "nutcracker" had been found. These objects indicated that the "nutcracker" might have been a toolmaker — that he might, in fact, have been the world's first.

At once, the "nutcracker" became a scientific celebrity

around the world. At first Dr. Leakey believed the skull belonged to a human being. Later he changed his mind. He decided that Zinjanthropus was a nonhuman. He guessed that the skull belonged to a member of an ancient species which long ago died out.

What, then, explains the tools found at Olduvai Gorge? If the "nutcracker" was not a human being, how could he have made and used tools at all?

This mystery deepened over the next five years as the Leakeys began piecing together bone fragments of still another ancient creature. This one, also discovered at Olduvai Gorge, was more humanlike in appearance than the "nutcracker." As Dr. Leakey explained it, this second creature probably lived about the same time as the "nutcracker." It may have been the first real toolmaker — and, according to Dr. Leakey, the first human.

Other experts have come up with different theories. But each of these theories has some built-in question marks of its own. And so, for the present, the Leakeys' findings might be compared to riddles written on the walls of time. We can see that the riddles are there, but we cannot yet be sure of what they mean.

We can nonetheless be certain of one thing: The detective work of Louis and Mary Leakey points to the conclusion that the human family tree first took root in Africa. And when you stop to think about it, that makes Africa the homeland not only of Africans but of every one of us on earth.

Double-check

Review

1. What do experts say is the total population of Africa?

2. African people make up what fraction of the world's population?

3. In what types of communities do the vast majority of Africans live?

4. Name three of the many groups of people who have long called Africa home.

5. Whom is Africa probably the homeland of?

Discussion

1. Chapter 2 tells us that scholars have sorted African people into a number of categories. What are some advantages of giving people these "identification tags"? What are some disadvantages?

2. What is the value of studying the origins of the human race, as the Leakeys have? What type of training would be useful for such work?

3. Chapter 1 points out that a Hollywood filmmaker would have a hard time trying to find "typical" African terrain. Why might the filmmaker also be hard pressed to find "typical" African people?

Activities

1. Some students might combine the information from the Population Distribution map with the information from the Land Use map and put this information, with the names of the major cities, on a large wall map.

2. Some authors have recently begun to use the name *Twa* instead of *Pygmies* when referring to this African ethnic group. Some students might research and report on the origins of each name and the reasons for and against making the change.

3. A committee of students might research a few of the major theories about the origins of the first humans, and then present their findings in a panel discussion.

Skills

READING MAPS OF AFRICA

Use the maps of Africa on pages 6, 25, and 27, and information in Chapter 2, to answer the following questions.

1. Most of West Africa lies where?
   (a) south of the Equator
   (b) south of the Tropic of Capricorn
   (c) south of the Tropic of Cancer

2. A more detailed map of Central Africa is located on what page?
   (a) page 41 (b) page 89 (c) page 6

3. Which section of Africa has no area classified as "uninhabited"?
   (a) Central Africa (b) East Africa (c) West Africa

4. In which section of Africa are there the most mountains?
   (a) North Africa (b) West Africa (c) East Africa

5. Which topic discussed in Chapter 2 is not illustrated on any of the three maps?
   (a) land use
   (b) population distribution
   (c) location of ethnic groups

Chapter 3

A Family Circle

FOR THE HUNDREDTH TIME, Nshombo* peered up the river. Here at Kinshasa,* the Zaïre River is so wide it resembles a huge lake. Looking upstream between the low-lying islands, Nshombo could see the river stretching all the way to the horizon. There was still no sign of the steamer that he was waiting for.

Nshombo's wife, Kaminda,* had gone back to her village three months ago to be with her own family for the birth of her first child. She and her newborn son were returning on the steamer which had been expected to dock early that morning. Now it was nearly two in the afternoon.

"Half a day late already," Nshombo thought. Then he shrugged. "Well, the steamers are always late. It will come."

He wiped the sweat from his face and neck. It was the middle of May, the last, but hottest, month of the rainy season. There were thundershowers almost every day, but the skies cleared quickly afterward, letting the sun blaze through again.

A few hundred yards from the dock, clumps of water plants were sweeping by on the muscle of the current. The tips of broken tree branches bobbed up and down as they passed. Nshombo watched one go by and wondered what would happen to it when it slammed into the rapids around the next bend. These rapids choke the Zaïre River below Kinshasa for 200 miles — not even the lightest dugout canoe can slip through. It is because Kinshasa is the last downstream stop for river traffic in Zaïre's interior that it has grown to be one of the largest and most important cities in Africa.

Suddenly the voices at one end of the dock grew louder. A woman, wrapping the loose end of her *lapa** — the large piece of cloth she used to form a skirt — around herself, stood and pointed out at the river. She looked back at the crowd.

"It's the steamer. I can see the smoke from the steamer's fire." Women from all over the dock came running over to the water's edge. Nshombo looked out over their heads. Smoke far off up the river was growing thicker and blacker.

Slowly the steamer drew closer. As it approached, Nshombo tried to see the faces of the passengers. On the top deck, he could pick out several men in white shirts and blue suits. These were probably government officials. There were also some officers of the Zaïrian National Army and a few Europeans. But Nshombo knew he would find his wife on the lower decks, which were still hidden by the ship's bow.

Gradually the steamer swung about. The propel-

"My son," Nshombo said. "My son." He turned to his wife, smiling. "We'll go home now."

lers churned up a brown stain as they fought against the current. For a moment, Nshombo saw his wife. He cried out, "Kaminda! Kaminda!" Then she was lost in the jumble of waving arms.

Five minutes later boarding planks were in place, and passengers began to cross over to the dock. Nshombo saw his wife and walked slowly toward her.

"Kaminda," he said. She held her head down but then looked up at him with bright eyes. Nshombo reached out and touched her on the cheek. Then he looked down at the tiny baby in her arms. He felt its head and fingers and pushed it lightly on the nose.

"My son," he said. "My son." He turned to his wife, smiling. "We'll go home now."

Behind one of the dock warehouses, Nshombo found an old, open truck with 10 or 12 men and women sitting on sacks of peanuts in the back. On the side of the truck a sign in roughly painted letters said: "Air Frambo." Frambo was the owner's name and he had added the "Air" to advertise the speed of his truck. It sounded a little like "Air Zaïre," the name of the national airline. On the other side of the truck, Mr. Frambo had painted: "God Help Us."

Nshombo learned that the truck was headed for the port city of Matadi.* To get to the Matadi Road, the driver had to pass near Nshombo's house. After some discussion, Nshombo and the driver agreed on 10 makuta* (about 20 cents) for the ride.

The truck bounced up a cobblestone street past warehouses and factories to the center of town. Here the avenues were lined with elegant shops and tall, modern apartment buildings. This section of Kinshasa, near the river, was built by Europeans for Europeans. Before Zaïre won its independence in 1960, only white people lived or shopped here. Now the Zaïrian people can live wherever they please. But only a few can afford the high prices of the European section.

The "Air Frambo" truck weaved its way through heavy traffic, down the palm-tree-lined main boulevard. Then it turned off the boulevard and raced toward another section of the sprawling Zaïrian city. Here there were few buildings more than two stories high. Tiny shops and bars and some brightly colored houses faced the avenue. Behind, on bumpy streets and alleyways of packed earth, were the endless rows of shacks where most Zaïrians in Kinshasa live. Nobody knows how many people live in this great city, but many thousands of Zaïrians have been drawn here from their villages by the hope of finding jobs. Nshombo scrambled over the sacks of peanuts and beat on the roof of the truck. "Let us off at the next corner. Bomboma* Street."

The truck whined to a stop, and Nshombo and Kaminda climbed out over the tailgate. Kaminda held the baby in one arm and placed the small bundle she had brought with her on her head. As they walked, Nshombo swung his arms out of pride while Kaminda followed timidly behind, baby in her arms, bundle on her head. In five minutes they were in the small cement courtyard belonging to Nshombo's father.

Mama na bana. *Mama na bana.* "Mother of children," Nshombo's mother said quietly as she greeted Kaminda. Kaminda's eyes sparkled as she heard the respectful words from her husband's mother. They shook hands loosely, without squeezing.

Other family members came over smiling to Ka-

To live off the land, African people must develop special skills. Here, a villager grates manioc* into flour.

❧ Nshombo's father and grandfather normally paid little attention to the talk of women.

minda, and each in turn shook hands. The women laughed and talked gaily as they examined the baby.

Finally, from a corner of the yard, Kaminda heard the voice of Nshombo's father: "Hey, what do you have over there?" And, with a broad grin, he too looked the baby over. Then he took Nshombo's hand and, leaving the women, led him over to a group of tables in the corner of the courtyard where six or seven men were drinking beer.

"My son," he told the men, "is now a father." He laughed, slapped Nshombo on the back, and called for someone to bring more beer.

Nshombo's father earned most of his living by selling beer at these few tables. To draw customers, he had written "International Bar" on the wall facing the street. At first he had called his bar the "Equateur,"* in honor of his native province. But he found that this name kept away people who came from other provinces.

Another source of money for Nshombo's father was the small cement houses that surrounded the courtyard. There were eight of these, each with two rooms. Family members lived in four of them, but the other four could be rented for the equivalent of a few dollars a month.

If a tenant decided the rent was too high, or chose to leave for another reason, Nshombo's father would ask him to stay rent-free until he found a replacement. For an empty house would soon attract another relative who could neither be turned away nor asked to pay rent. The relatives in the houses now —

Nshombo and Kaminda, Nshombo's grandfather, sister, and half sister — earned their keep by cooking and doing other chores. One of the girls was training to be a policewoman, and the other sold home-roasted peanuts to customers of the International Bar. They often bought food and contributed it to family meals. So did Nshombo, who worked in a print shop.

It was now dusk, and the women busied themselves around the cooking fire. The usual meal was a pasty dish made from the thick white root of the manioc plant. The root is ground into flour, mixed with water, molded, and sliced. The slices are dropped into a hot, spicy vegetable sauce and cooked. Nshombo's family usually ate vegetables also: manioc leaves, corn and beans, and rice, and often fish either dried or freshly caught from the river.

Tonight, to celebrate the return of his wife and baby, Nshombo had bought a chicken to use in a favorite Zaïrian dish known as *moambe.* * The women cooked the chicken in palm oil with palm nuts and served it with shredded coconut meat, sliced papaya, bananas, avocados, and other fruits.

"Tell us news of your family and village," Nshombo's father asked Kaminda when they had finished eating. "We have received no letters from the village in some time."

Although Nshombo and Kaminda had first met in Kinshasa, their families came from villages near each other in Equateur Province. Kaminda knew that the members of Nshombo's family were most interested in their own village and the relatives who had remained there. She talked shyly of what she had seen and heard. One of Nshombo's uncles had taken a new wife. Another had had to rebuild his hut after a bad rainstorm. An aunt had offended the spirit of her dead father and had taken a bad fall, but amends had been made by the sacrifice of a sheep. The corn was tall, with many ears — a good crop. Kaminda even remembered the names of all the families with new babies.

Nshombo's father and grandfather normally paid little attention to the talk of women, but now they listened carefully to every piece of news. They would have made Kaminda talk all night if a sudden rain hadn't put out the fire and driven them inside to bed.

Double-check

Review

1. Why is Kinshasha one of Africa's largest and most important cities?

2. What are makuta?

3. When did Zaïre win its independence?

4. Why have many thousands of Zaïrian villagers been drawn to Kinshasha?

5. Why did Nshombo's father first call his bar the "Equateur"? Why did he change the name?

Discussion

1. When Kaminda and the baby came home, Nshombo's family celebrated by having a special meal. When are special meals an important part of celebrating in your home? Why is food used for celebrations almost everywhere?

2. What could or should the government of Zaïre do about the thousands of villagers who come to Kinshasha looking for jobs — give them housing? Find them jobs? Stop them from coming?

3. In Nshombo's family, everyone worked inside or outside the home to support the family. Is such economic cooperation as important — or as common — in families in the U.S. as it is in Zaïre? Explain your answer.

Activities

1. Some students might research and report to the rest of the class on the custom of using food and special meals as a form of celebration — in Africa, in the U.S., and in other countries.

2. A few students might role-play a conversation between Nshombo's father and some relatives who come to stay in one of his apartments. He doesn't need their cooking or help around the house, but they have no money for rent. Nshombo's father must decide whether to let them stay and, if so, on what terms.

3. Someone who has studied or visited Zaïre might be invited to speak to the class about life in that country.

Skills

USING AN INDEX

Zaïre, 37–45, 93–105, 139,*
  148,* 174
Zaïre River, 37–39, 170
Zaïre River Basin, 14
Zaïrian National Army, 38
Zambezi River, 134,* 170
Zambia, 109
Zanzibar, 170
Zima, Peter, 207–217
Zimbabwe, 153,* 191, 198,
  199, 204
Zinjanthropus, 33–34
Zulu (language), 56

*Photograph

Use the index listings above and information in Chapter 3 to answer the following questions.

1. In what order are topics listed in an index?
   (a) order of importance   (b) alphabetical order   (c) page numbers

2. On how many pages is the Zaïre River mentioned?
   (a) three   (b) 37   (c) four

3. On which page will you find a photograph of Peter Zima?
   (a) page 207   (b) page 217   (c) none

4. On which page is Zaïre last mentioned in this book?
   (a) page 139   (b) page 174   (c) page 58

5. On which page would you find a photo of people in the city in which Nshombo lives?
   (a) page 148   (b) page 139   (c) page 170

2
TRADITIONAL
AFRICA

Chapter 4

Roots of Civilization

NOWHERE IN THE WORLD can humans escape nature's influence. Sun, rain, wind, soil — all these have affected people in a variety of ways. Like most of the world's millions, the people of Tropical and Southern Africa have lived close to nature. Over the centuries they have struggled day by day and year by year to tame the land and bring it under control.

Living in huts made of mud and thatch, drawing food from the unpredictable earth, African farmers cannot help but be influenced by the land around them. They are themselves a part of the land, and the land affects almost everything they say and do.

On days when the sun is warm and the crops are green, African farmers have reason to give thanks to nature. But throughout African history, nature has been a fickle friend, sometimes bestowing its gifts, sometimes suddenly withdrawing them. Along with

49

◄§ No one could be certain of what lay ahead, but some people could try to guess — and did.

---

bountiful harvests, it has brought droughts, floods, famines, and disease. For Africans such hardships have often seemed all the more painful because they have been so difficult to explain.

To help explain their hardships, Africans long ago developed their own religious beliefs. At the center was the belief that all events were the work of unseen but powerful forces present throughout nature. These forces could be found, for example, in trees, rivers, mountains, and streams.

In the traditional belief, every happening — even the softest chirping of a bird — could be traced to the spirit world. When things went well, Africans believed the spirits were rewarding humans with favor. When things went badly, the spirits were punishing them for the errors of their ways. Since the spirits had so much power, they had to be respected. Thus, African villagers often said prayers and performed sacrifices to honor these spirits and enlist their sympathy and support.

Such beliefs — called animism* in English — came to dominate the thinking of more than half of the continent. But the details of these beliefs differ widely from village to village and ethnic group to ethnic group. Each group had its own spirits and its own ceremonies for paying them respect. And each group

Farmers of Mali try to predict the future by drawing diagrams in the sand. During the night foxes run over the diagrams. In the morning, men try to read the future by the fox tracks.*

developed its own notions about how men should conduct themselves in their daily lives.

But no matter how their faiths differed, most Africans in traditional society held certain basic religious views. They believed that some spirits had more power than others. The mightiest was a remote but all-powerful Supreme Being, little concerned with the daily affairs of men. Under this Supreme Being there were often the spirits which commanded natural elements such as sun, water, and wind. Finally, there were the souls of the ancestors.

Why ancestors? Like many other people, African villagers believed the human spirit was immortal. In their view, the human soul lived on after death, making its "home" amid the forces of the spirit world. In time, each soul was thought to return to the village where it had once lived. Since the soul remained in touch with the spirits, it served as a go-between for humans and the spirit world.

As go-betweens, the ancestral spirits were powerful and commanded the respect and reverence of the people. Especially important were the spirits of the community's founders. Yet the reasons for African ancestor worship went deeper than the simple fear of the power of the spirits. In everything they did, Africans believed themselves to be a link in a chain of life which included the spirits of the dead and the spirits of people still to be born.

Thus, Africans in a traditional society lived in a well-ordered world where almost everything had an explanation. No one could be certain of what lay ahead, but some people could try to guess — and did. The guesswork was usually left to spiritual experts who were thought to have special powers. These powers helped them to communicate more directly with the spirit world.

Their most important task was to stand watch over the religious well-being of the people. They did so mainly by supervising local ceremonies in honor of the spirits. Through such ceremonies they hoped to win spiritual favor and control the course of natural events. Out of their ceremonies grew many accomplishments in art and music which enriched African life.

In preparing these ceremonies, for example, Africans usually created special costumes to stand for the spirits being honored. These costumes often included head masks and highly ornamented skirts. Priests would sometimes make these costumes sacred by inviting the spirit to dwell within them. Yet even the most sacred costumes remained symbols of the spirits and never became objects of worship in themselves.

In this colorful and lively artwork, Africans captured many of their own attitudes toward the spirits. Many head masks depicted the emotions of the spirits — their kindliness or cruelty, their vanity or rage. Some masks were meant to picture the power of nature. Used in a dance or ritual, they gave the occasion a special enchantment, as though the spirits themselves were really there.

Costumes and masks gave ceremonies added excitement, and music added movement and direction. With its emphasis on rhythm, African music was designed for dancing, which became an art in itself. Unlike other types of dancing, most African religious dancing was carefully staged. Much of it was as elaborate as a European ballet.

In actual performance, however, these dances had the appearance of being completely unplanned. Dancers became shadows in the fading firelight, moving to the pulse of drums. As they went through their motions, they attempted to lose themselves in the dance. At the climax of the ritual, they were thought to be at one with the spirit world.

Such ceremonies were a basic part of traditional life. In much of Africa they still are. Over the course of centuries many of the people of Tropical and Southern Africa have become Moslems or Christians (see Chapter 10). Yet six out of 10 Africans today still follow animist beliefs.

In doing so, they are paying tribute to the land which has given them life itself. As an old saying of the Mossi* people of Upper Volta has it: "Land is the mother, it fed the ancestors of this generation; it feeds the present generation and its children; and it provides the final resting place for all men."

☆   ☆   ☆   ☆   ☆   ☆   ☆   ☆   ☆

The land which has given Africans life has also influenced their social customs. The influence reaches right down to the languages they speak. Since most African villagers make their living off the land, they have built their traditions in relative isolation. In the process, they have developed the most bewildering array of languages anywhere in the world.

This has created a language barrier which exists even at the local level. In some cases villagers living only a few hundred yards from one another find it hard to communicate without an interpreter. Such a problem — bothersome enough in a small village — becomes vastly magnified on a national scale. There are very few African countries in which one language is spoken by all of the people. And in the West African country of Nigeria, people speak some 250 different tongues.

All in all, Africa has at least 800 distinct languages. Most are tonal — that is, most have words which carry different meanings when said in different

◦§ Most religious dancing was carefully staged. Much of it was as elaborate as a European ballet.

Among traditional Africans such as these Ewe villagers, dancing is still considered a high art. Often it is part of a religious ritual believed to honor the forces of the spirit world.

tones of voice. Before the coming of the Europeans to the continent about two centuries ago, few African languages were written. Africa did have its own literature, but nearly all of it was passed along by word of mouth.

Scholars group the traditional African languages into four main categories:

*Niger-Congo.** This group of languages, spoken throughout the southern half of the continent, is the largest of the four groups. Two of the most common Niger-Congo languages are Swahili* (spoken in the east) and Zulu* (spoken in the south).

*Sudanic.** The Sudanic languages make up the second largest group. They are generally confined to the grasslands just south of the Sahara.

Afro-Asiatic. As their name implies, the Afro-Asiatic languages are also spoken in the Middle East. In Tropical Africa, they are spoken in parts of the northern section. They include Hausa* (one of the most common languages of West Africa) and Amharic* (the official tongue of Ethiopia).

*Khoisan.** This language family can be easily identified by the tongue clicks which are a distinctive part of its speech. The Khoisan languages are spoken by some people in southern Africa and by a few in the eastern nation of Tanzania.

Since there are so many African languages, an African who leaves his or her village must often speak two — or more — languages. To hurdle the communications barrier, Africans often use so-called "trade languages" — languages spoken by a large enough group of people to serve as a common tongue. Of the traditional African languages, two in particular serve as trade languages — Swahili in East Africa and Hausa in the West. In addition, many Africans now speak one or another of the European languages —

especially English, French, and Portuguese — which were introduced into Africa during the colonial period (see page 168).

Trade languages help build bridges between Africa's many ethnic groups. Thus far, however, they are not common enough to bring unity to the entire continent. As the variety of languages shows, Tropical and Southern Africa has not one but many cultures. And each of these cultures has its own enduring customs and beliefs.

Double-check

Review

1. What idea lies at the center of Africans' animist religious beliefs?

2. Why are the spirits of dead ancestors important to living Africans?

3. What was the most important task of spiritual leaders in Africa?

4. About how many distinct languages are there in Africa?

5. What is a trade language?

Discussion

1. Why might people choose to worship "spirits" that seem to control the sun, wind, and water?

2. How do the religious practices of traditional Africans differ from those in your community? In what ways are they similar?

3. Should each African nation adopt one official language for all of its citizens to write and speak? Why, or why not? If so, how could this be done?

Activities

1. An African language expert might be invited to speak to the class. He or she could discuss basic differences in various languages, and perhaps teach students a few greetings in a trade language.

2. Students might attend a local performance of African dance or, with the aid of a dance instructor from the school or community, they might participate in a classroom demonstration of an African religious dance.

3. Much of Africa's history has not been written, but passed along by word of mouth. Students might conduct their own oral history projects — by talking to older citizens about the history of their communities or to older relatives about important events in the history of their families.

Skills

READERS' GUIDE TO PERIODICAL LITERATURE

March 1977—February 1978

page 10

AFRICA (continued)
Economic conditions
Air transport can help strengthen Africa's economy, ICAO study finds. UN Chron 14:30-1 Mr '77
Developing states of Africa. R. S. Morgenthau. bibl f Ann Am Acad 432:80-95 Jl '77
See also
United Nations—Economic Commission for Africa

page 11

Languages
See also
Bantu languages
Swahili language
Maps
Map section. Sr Schol 110:29 O 20 '77
Native races
See also
Pygmies
Politics and government
Political transition in urban Africa; Mushin sector of Lagos, Nigeria. S. T. Barnes. bibl f Ann Am Acad 432:26-41 Jl '77
See also
Organization of African Unity
Religious institutions and affairs
Church in Africa: from adolescence to maturity; interview, ed by H. Lindsell, G. B. Osei-Mensah. por Chr Today 21:17-19 Ja 7 '77
Reappraisal of polygamy in Africa. P. Bock. bibl il Intellect 105:435-6 Je '77

Abbreviations

Ann Am Acad—*Annals of the American Academy of Political and Social Science*

bibl — bibliography

bibl f — bibliographical footnotes

Chr Today — *Christianity Today*

ICAO — International Civil Aviation Organization

il — illustrated

Ja — January

Je — June

Jl — July

Mr — March

O — October

por — portrait

Sr Schol — *Senior Scholastic*

Un Chron — *UN Chronicle*

Use the above listings from Readers' Guide to Periodical Literature *and information in Chapter 4 to answer the following questions.*

1. Which magazine listed above has a portrait accompanying an article?

2. This volume of *Readers' Guide* will have listings of magazine articles that appeared in print in January of what year?

3. How many magazine articles on African economic conditions are listed above?

4. Which magazine listed above has a map section on Africa?

5. Under what category in this volume of *Readers' Guide* should one look to find an article about one of the African languages mentioned in Chapter 4?

Chapter 5

Family, Clan, Community, Nation

HOWEVER ELSE they may differ, the villagers of Tropical and Southern Africa are a social people. They live in groups, work in groups, and share their experiences in many ways. All this togetherness arises partly from a need for protection in a world that is sometimes hostile. An old West African proverb sums up the situation: "If one tree gets all the wind, it will break."

In Tropical and Southern Africa, the main "windbreaker" is the family. In times of crisis, it is to their families that Africans usually turn. In Africa, the family — not the individual — comes first. For that reason, villagers are taught the importance of the family almost from birth.

For the African villager, that birth is likely to occur in a hut made of mud and thatch. Like babies everywhere, the African infant lives in a world peopled by a few familiar faces — father and mother, brothers and sisters. These people make up the *nuclear* family — that is, the family's most immediate core.

As the child grows older, the number of family faces increases rapidly. By the time the child has reached the age of four, he or she is expected to know all the kinfolk — aunts and uncles, cousins, and grandparents. The family circle may be even wider. If the father is a wealthy man, he may practice polygyny* — the taking of several wives at once. One out of every 10 men in Tropical and Southern Africa follows this custom. But it is usually reserved for the well-to-do, who can afford to feed the extra mouths.

Poorer families often double up in a different way. Brothers frequently share a single dwelling, called a compound, along with their wives, children, and parents. Such an arrangement might seem strange to us. Yet Africans don't think so. Family ties are so strong that Africans consider such a group to be fairly small and anything much smaller to be downright antisocial.

As the young person becomes more aware of the family, he or she learns that the welfare of the whole family comes before the welfare of its individual members. One reason is that the family is a part of the religious belief, since it serves as a link between ancestors and those yet unborn.

Week by week the child's world widens like the ripples in a pool. Gradually the child becomes aware of the mountains or plains, forests or fields which lie beyond the village huts. The child learns to distinguish manioc from millet, porcupines from wild pigs. As this happens, the world of the village and the world outside the village blend slowly into one.

By the time a child is six, he or she has begun to carry out a few of the family's chores. A girl, for example, may be gathering and cooking food. A boy may be tending the family's calves and goats. At about this age, young people begin to mingle with the older people of the village. Through this, they get to know some of the more distant members of their clans.

The clan is a group of people who trace their descent back to a single ancestor. Most villages are made up of members of several clans. The clan, in turn, may be spread across three or four villages or it may be much, much larger. The largest clans, like those within the Ibo* or Yoruba* groups of West Africa, may number as many as half a million people.

Members of a clan often believe they have a special link to one animal or object — a zebra, for example, or an elephant. They have adopted this animal or object as the symbol of their clan. They call themselves members of the Zebra Clan or the Elephant Clan or whatever — and all who belong to this clan are thought to be their brothers.

Once young people have learned about their clan, they are ready to take their place in a still larger group — their political community. Such communities are organized in a number of different ways. Many are ruled by chiefs, who inherit their jobs from their fathers or brothers. Many chiefs lead by means of councils, which make decisions after long debates.

Chiefs and councillors have to respect the traditions of their people. Failure to do so may bring dismissal. In addition, such leaders are expected to unite their subjects and rally them to a common purpose. For it is this sense of shared purpose which helps to hold the chiefdom together.

Sometimes a number of chiefdoms form a still larger community. This type of community is bound together by even broader ties. Its members may

☙ Having more than one wife is usually reserved for the well-to-do, who can afford to feed the extra mouths.

When is a family too large — or not large enough? This village chief has several wives and a crowd of children. What advantages do you see in this family arrangement? What drawbacks?

Can you write your own caption for this photo
of a village chief in Ghana? Look at the
picture closely. What is the chief doing? Who
are the people around him? How might the photo
show Africans' respect for village traditions?

◄§ Village chiefs are expected to unite their subjects and rally them to a common purpose.

speak the same language, for example, or they may share the same customs. Or they may do both.

All these communities make African society complex. Outsiders have commonly simplified their explanations of this society by referring to many of its groups as "tribes." But many educated Africans argue that the word "tribe" has no precise meaning. They say that to apply it only to Africans is to give the false impression that Africans are more sharply divided along ethnic lines than people in other parts of the world.

In any event, young people in traditional African villages must often prepare themselves to live in several kinds of communities at once. The full meaning of these communities first becomes clear about the time these young people reach their teens. At that age they are usually packed off to "cult schools," often located outside the village. Far from the eyes of curious villagers, they are put to many tests of skill and daring. Day by day the suspense mounts until, finally, it ends in an awesome climax. This is the ritual of initiation into adulthood — the most important event of a young person's life.

Perhaps the most exciting of these rituals is the lion hunt conducted among male members of the Masai* community of East Africa. This event has now become far less common than it once was — but it sometimes still takes place. It occurs when a Masai boy has reached the age of 13. Armed with a shield and a spear, he must kill a lion to prove he is a man.

The boy has grown up with a spear and has probably longed for this day as long as he can remember. Together, the warriors and the boy move through the tall, golden brush toward the lion and surround him. The boy edges his way through the circle. The lion's tail snaps back and forth angrily, and he bares his fangs in a deep-throated growl. Too late he seeks a break in the circle through which he can flee.

Now there come shouts and a stamping of feet. Metal bracelets jangle. Headdresses bob up and down. The Masai close in tighter, their brightly decorated shields held ready. The boy runs forward. The lion crouches to leap.

Then, flashing through the bright African sun, arches the famous Masai spear — slender as a needle, dipped traditionally in cattle blood. As the spear strikes home, 25 other spears, held in stronger hands, wait to be guided to the same target. But the boy must strike the fatal blow.

Few African initiation rituals are as exciting, or as dangerous, as this one. In fact, such rituals vary from one African community to the next. In some areas, these rituals are not even practiced. And in some of the areas where they have been practiced for centuries, they are today slowly dying out.

But the rituals that are still practiced all have one thing in common. They provide a test of courage and skill. By giving young people a chance to prove their worth, they prepare them for the responsibilities of adulthood.

The next concern of young Africans is likely to be a hunt of a very different sort — the hunt for a suitable marriage partner. Among some groups of Tropical Africa, in fact, this hunt begins before young people enter their teens. As soon as they are old enough to leave the village, they tag along with their parents on trips to nearby market towns. There they concen-

◄§ Today national boundaries often separate people of the same ethnic groups.

From time to time disputes break out between neighboring African ethnic groups. When they do, women and children are often caught in the middle of bloody conflict. The photo shows Somali* refugees fleeing from Kenya into Somalia.*

trate on making new friends, especially friends of the opposite sex.

Why travel so far afield? Doing so simply makes it easier to meet people from outside one's own clan. A clan is a group of relatives, remember, and custom among many groups of Tropical Africa forbids marrying another member of the same clan.

Such journeys may go on for several years before young people are old enough to wed. That age may be anywhere from the midteens to the late twenties, depending on the group (for the example of the Kikuyu* people, see Chapter 11). When the two young people are old enough (and when both families consent to the union), the marriage may occur. Festivities may be short and businesslike, or they may go on for several days. They are likely to last the longest when families have traveled great distances in order to attend.

When the celebrating ends, the bride and groom go back to their hut or compound, there to begin raising a family of their own. Most Africans believe that it is of great importance to bear children, and failure to do so is often a mark of some disgrace (see Chapter 6). For children add to the "wealth" of an African family and serve as its link with the future. Without children, the system could not endure.

And endure it has. Down through the centuries it has involved African villagers in a vast maze of relationships with a meaning all their own. Traditionally, these villagers have been taught to give their loyalty to their families, clans, and communities. And nowadays most of them are also expected to be loyal to the newly created nations to which they belong.

These nations have generally been carved out of former colonial territories (see page 168). Often their national boundaries do not match the ethnic boundaries of the Africans themselves. For example, the Hausas — one of West Africa's largest groups — are spread across parts of both Nigeria and Niger. In East Africa, wandering Somali herdsmen often cross borders between Somalia, Ethiopia (to the north), and Kenya (to the south).

Nor do a nation's laws always conform to the laws of the traditional villages. Over the past two decades Africa's various national governments have worked out their own legal codes, based largely on former colonial laws. Again and again these legal codes have conflicted with older ways of thinking. In the process, they have created bitter clashes between the old and the new.

Some African leaders have called for a loosening of traditional bonds among their people. These leaders believe that local communities divide the loyalties of the people and thereby weaken their sense of national unity. And they believe that national unity is the key to Africa's strength in the modern world.

But many other Africans take issue with this argument. They point out that the traditional villages have been the keystone of African life for centuries. Many agree that Africa must look to the future. But they maintain that it must do so without destroying all the foundations of the past.

Just to the south of the enormous Sahara sits Timbuktu, once the center for early empires of the Western Sudan.

TURNING GOLD
TO SALT

MORE THAN 10 CENTURIES AGO, camel caravans first inched across the vast Sahara, fragile outlines arched against the bright desert sky. They came and went in small groups, slowly tramping through the searing sun and blinding sand. Their journeys sometimes lasted for weeks and were dangerous at best. In an age not given to long-distance traveling, these desert crossings stood out boldly as a mark of Africa on the move.

The men who did the moving were Arabs from North Africa. They were bound for the Western Sudan, a grassy region which stretched from the southwestern edge of the Sahara to the rain forests along the Gulf of Guinea (*see map on page 72*). What lured these travelers into the Western Sudan? The answer was gold. In time they helped to turn parts of the area into commercial centers.

The basic reasons for the trade were simple enough. Though Western Sudanese farmers could provide their people with food, their soil did not yield one of the main staples of diet — salt. So the Western Sudanese had to get their salt from elsewhere. And "elsewhere" was the salt mines in what is now Morocco and Algeria.

Arab traders could bring salt to the Western Sudanese. But what could the farmers give the traders in return? As it happened, the Western Sudanese controlled the traffic in gold. Experts do not agree on where this gold came from, but the best guess seems to be the region between the sources of the Senegal* and Niger rivers. In any event, the Western Sudanese had more than enough gold to trade for all the salt they needed.

Over the course of centuries the traffic in gold and salt enriched the Arab traders. But it had a far greater impact on the various people of the Western Sudan. Between 700 A.D. and 1700 A.D., this trade prompted the rise of three great Western Sudanese kingdoms — Ghana, Mali, and Songhay.* And it enabled these kingdoms to reach a level of achievement that was comparable with many European states of the time.

The earliest of these so-called "gold-salt" empires was Ghana. Some historians trace its origins back as far as the fourth century A.D. Yet it wasn't until about 700 A.D. that the leadership of Ghana fell to a black people known as the Soninkes.* And it wasn't until the Soninkes took control that the glory of Ghana really began.

The Soninkes were not one group, but a number of related people, all of whom spoke a language called Mande.* The Soninkes developed a reputation as fearsome fighters. In battle they had an edge over their opponents, for they are believed to have been the first Western Sudanese people to use weapons made of iron. Over several centuries they used this advantage to extend the

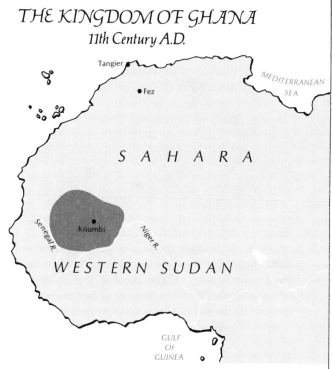

THE KINGDOM OF GHANA
11th Century A.D.

Tangier

Fez

MEDITERRANEAN SEA

S A H A R A

Senegal R.

Koumbi

Niger R.

W E S T E R N   S U D A N

GULF OF GUINEA

boundaries of their empire all the way from the Niger River in the south into the Sahara in the north.

While the Ghanaians* were enlarging their territory, they were expanding in other ways as well. In particular, they were turning their capital of Koumbi* into a hub of commerce which attracted merchandise from far and wide. From the north came wheat. From the south came cattle, sheep, and honey. And there was a wealth of other goods — raisins, cloth, leather goods — from many places.

Gold, of course, was their most valuable source of wealth, and the Ghanaians tried their best to hoard it. No one except the king was allowed to own gold in nugget form. By keeping these nuggets scarce, the Ghanaians probably believed they would keep the value of gold high. Yet the king was allowed to use his gold in any way he saw fit, and apparently he did so. According to one account, he even put the metal into collars for his dogs.

Such displays of wealth did wonders for Ghana's trade.

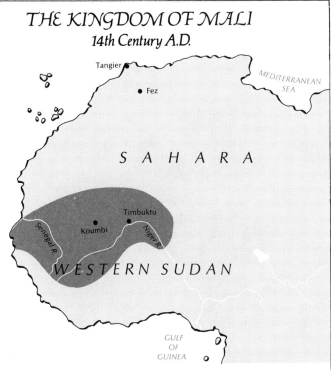

THE KINGDOM OF MALI
14th Century A.D.

Tangier

Fez

MEDITERRANEAN SEA

S A H A R A

Timbuktu

Koumbi

Senegal R.

Niger R.

WESTERN SUDAN

GULF OF GUINEA

As trade expanded, Ghana's merchants prospered. The kingdom grew richer and more powerful until the 1060's. Then it was hit by an invasion of Moslems from the north and, like a house of cards, the empire crumbled.

From the ashes of one empire grew the beginnings of another. This second "gold-salt empire" was Mali, ruled by a people known as the Mandingoes.* The Mandingoes were distant relatives of the Soninkes and spoke the same language, Mande. Back in the 11th century, however, the two groups had taken separate religious paths. While the Soninkes remained animists, the Mandingoes had been converted to the religion of Islam.

Like the Soninkes, the Mandingoes were great warriors. They extended their empire through a series of wars topped off by the capture of Koumbi in 1240 A.D. As successors to the Soninkes, the Mandingoes took control of the gold-salt trade. Then they transferred that trade to their own cities, especially the fabled Timbuktu.*

THE KINGDOM OF SONGHAY
16th Century A.D.

Timbuktu had been established in the area where the Niger River begins to bend southward toward the sea. Under the Mandingoes the city became a major crossroads of trade. As time went on, it also became a center of Moslem learning.

Timbuktu reached the height of its power in the reign of a mansa* (or sultan) named Musa.* Mansa Musa reached the throne in 1307 and ruled until 1332. His most famous exploit was a pilgrimage he made from Timbuktu to the Moslem holy city of Mecca on the Arabian Peninsula. On his thousand-mile journey he reportedly took along a caravan large enough to cause a traffic jam even in the desolate Sahara. According to some estimates, the size of his party numbered an astonishing 60,000 people.

To keep this procession traveling in style, the emperor is said to have carried more than 20,000 pounds of gold dust, which he generously proceeded to give away at many stops en route. By the time he made his trip homeward, he had handed out so much gold that he had to take a loan to complete the journey. Tales of his generosity spread across the Middle East, making Timbuktu seem the wealthiest city in the world.

Shortly after Mansa Musa's death in 1332, Timbuktu was captured by a band of warriors from the south. Then the kingdom of Mali began to slide downhill. At about the same time a third empire was already in the making. It was known by the people who ruled it — the Songhays.

Though their origin is unknown, the Songhays had long farmed and fished along the banks of the Niger River. During the 14th century they had been subjects of the emperor of Mali. In the middle of the next century they rose up and overthrew their former overlords. Then they took control of the gold-salt trade for themselves.

Again the boundaries of empire widened. The borders of Songhay eventually took in a territory almost the size of Europe. To police their far-flung lands, the Songhays kept a strong army. They are also believed to have created an elaborate central government.

Their greatest emperor was Askia Mohammed,* who took the throne in 1493. This devout Moslem made the city of Timbuktu an even greater center of Islamic culture than it had been under the Mandingoes of Mali. He too made a journey to Mecca which rivaled the pilgrimage of Mansa Musa nearly two centuries earlier. In many ways Askia Mohammed gave the Western Sudanese their most glorious moments of all.

Then, once again, a Western Sudanese empire fell into decline. The end came in 1591 when cannon-toting Moors of Morocco invaded Songhay and defeated its armies. For centuries thereafter the Western Sudanese remained a nearly forgotten people. Timbuktu became a password for a jumping-off place to nowhere — romantic, distant, isolated.

Only in recent years have historians given the accomplishments of Ghana, Mali, and Songhay the respect due them. Restored to their proper place in today's textbooks, those accomplishments are proof that West Africa was alive and well long before the rise of modern Europe.

Double-check

Review

1. For what reason are African villagers taught the importance of the family at an early age?

2. What is a nuclear family?

3. What is a clan?

4. Why might a lion hunt be an important event to a young Masai boy?

5. More than 10 centuries ago, what goods did Western Sudanese people trade with Arabs from North Africa?

Discussion

1. This chapter points out that many national boundaries in Africa do *not* match the ancient ethnic boundaries because they were carved out of former colonial territories. Should these boundaries be changed now?

2. What tests for adulthood are practiced in your community? In what ways are they like the Masai lion hunt? How are they different?

3. This chapter shows that historians sometimes leave important facts (such as the stories of Ghana, Mali, and Songhay) out of their books. Why don't historians record all events? How should they decide what to include and what to leave out?

Activities

1. If possible, your class might pretend that you are writing a history of your community. List 10 events that have occurred in your lifetime that you should be sure to include in the history. After you and fellow historians (classmates) compare lists, the class might vote on the 10 most important events to be included in the history. Discuss the reasons why some events will be included and others omitted.

2. The class might pretend that it is an African village. Then two students might role-play the parts of African leaders trying to persuade the village to loosen its traditional ties to families and clans so that it may become more loyal to the national government. Two other students might present arguments against such a change. After an informal debate, the rest of the class should vote on what the village will do.

3. Some students might research and report on various aspects of the cultures of one or more of the ancient African civilizations that existed before the growth of Western civilizations.

Skills

WEST AFRICAN CIVILIZATIONS

1240 A.D.	A. Mansa Musa ruled the Mali Kingdom.
1493 A.D.	B. Ghana Empire destroyed by Moslem invaders.
	C. Askia Muhammed ruled in Timbuktu.
700 A.D.	D. Camel caravans first crossed the Sahara.
1591 A.D.	E. Moroccan Moors defeated the armies of Songhai.
10,000 years ago	F. Ghana Empire first led by the Soninkes.
	G. Mandingoes captured the city of Koumbi.
1307 A.D.	
1060's A.D.	

Use the two lists above and information in Chapter 5 to do the following on a separate sheet of paper.

1. On the left side of your paper, make a vertical column of the dates given above, putting the dates in chronological order. (The dates are *not* in correct order above.)

2. Using the dates and clues in the chapter, write each event above next to the year or time period in which the event happened. (The events are *not* in the correct order in the list above.)

Chapter 6

A Broken String

KASSI* LOCKED THE DOOR of his brick-making shop and stepped out into the hot morning sun. Squinting up the dusty street he saw that a large crowd had already gathered in front of the house of the village chief.

"Come on, Mother. It's beginning," Kassi called impatiently to the old woman fussing in a nearby doorway.

"Yes. Well, moving slowly won't stop us from arriving," she answered. "There is time. A week from tonight you'll still be dancing."

Kassi laughed, and a feeling of happy excitement surged through him. At last his mother and father and old Uncle Aka* came out of the square yellow house. Chatting gaily, they turned up the street toward the clamor of the festival.

For as long as he could remember, Kassi had liked the festival of the yams better than any other time of the year. Like the other young men of his Ivory Coast village, he looked forward most to the nights of dancing and feasting. But he also loved the happy, carefree spirit that festival time brought to his Agni* people. The yam harvest was in, and each family had stored away enough of the starchy roots to fill all stomachs for many months. It was a time to give thanks to God and nature and to celebrate the start of a new year.

"It's a good week, this one, for doing certain things," Kassi's mother told him teasingly. "I hope you won't waste it chasing some of those silly girls I've seen you with. It's time you found a serious woman who could give us some fat grandchildren. What about that pretty Amah,* Boa's daughter?"

"Oh, she is very beautiful. And she seems to have good habits. But she scarcely looks at me."

"You and your brick money are the best catch in the village," Kassi's mother went on. "It would surprise me if greedy old Boa hasn't already told his daughter to smile at you tonight."

Kassi answered her with an embarrassed laugh.

The shouting and laughing of the crowd suddenly quieted. Kassi looked up to see the old chief emerging from his house. Although dressed in an elegant robe of gay colors, the chief's expression was stern, as if to remind his people that there was also a solemn side of the yam festival.

Now the villagers began to move past the chief's house toward the edge of the deep forest which surrounded their town. They threaded their way between two mahogany trees onto a well-worn path leading down to the river. Kassi left his family to join some other young men near the head of the procession.

The festival ceremonies began at the edge of the

river. The people gave thanks to the spirits of peace and fertility, and rejoiced in the abundance of their crops. One of the local leaders stood and recited the history of the village. Then, to renew themselves for the year ahead, the villagers bathed in the river, the women in a special place downstream.

Once, Kassi caught a glimpse of Amah. She was returning from her river bath, her face and arms still glistening from the water as she hugged her robe tightly around her. "Yes," Kassi said to himself, "Amah is very beautiful. Perhaps I should take my mother's advice."

During the dancing on the third night, Kassi finally found the courage to approach Amah. She was sitting alone.

"I am amazed to see that such a beautiful flower is not surrounded by a swarm of admirers," Kassi said with a flourish.

"Your silly compliments would perhaps work better with those other flowers," Amah replied, nodding her head toward a group of girls giggling nearby. But then she looked up at Kassi and smiled. Confused and embarrassed, he dropped with a crash into the chair beside her.

When Kassi began to talk again, it was in his normal, serious manner. He spoke of village affairs and told Amah of his brick business.

"I've heard about your bricks," Amah said. "My father says that the government's new building projects in this region will make you a rich man. Is it true?"

Kassi was pleased and flattered by Amah's interest. For a moment he remembered his mother's remarks about how Boa, Amah's father, would probably urge his daughter to smile at him.

"Still," Kassi said to himself, "she is a very beautiful girl."

A goat, a lamb, and a pot of grain were the gifts which this West African husband gave his bride's family on his wedding day. How does this tradition compare with U.S. wedding customs? Does the bride's family or the groom's family usually bear most wedding costs in the U.S.?

꩜ "My coming here is more than just a friendly visit," Kassi's uncle began. "I bring you a message of great importance from Kassi. He tells me that the cure for his sickness can be found in your house."

Kassi and Amah saw each other often during the days and nights of the festival. They danced together, and bit by bit their conversation became less formal. The words they spoke were those of a young man and woman who had grown fond of each other.

Late in May, just as the heavy summer rains began to fall, Kassi talked with his family about Amah. He told how he had been meeting with her for four months, ever since the yam festival. Then he announced his intention to marry her.

"Well, we're not surprised," his father laughed. "We didn't think that your visits to her village were for selling bricks."

"It's a good marriage," Kassi's mother said. "You will have our blessings."

Most African marriages represent an agreement between two families, rather than simply an agreement between two people. Sometimes, although it is rare today, families may arrange a marriage without even consulting the bride. Normally, however, the girl and boy reach an understanding between themselves before their families negotiate the terms of their marriage.

It was agreed that Uncle Aka would visit Boa's family to ask for Amah's hand. He set out the next day with a bottle of gin, the customary Agni offering for this occasion.

Old Boa greeted Aka with a sly smile. He pretended not to know the purpose of the visit and made polite talk about the weather and crops. Finally Aka came to the point.

"My coming here is more than just the friendly visit of a neighbor," Kassi's uncle began. "I bring you a message of great importance from my nephew, Kassi, the brick-maker. He has for several months been suffering from a strange illness which causes his mind to stray from his work. He tells me that the cure for this sickness can be found in your house."

Aka enjoyed this sort of speechmaking. He went on speaking in flowery phrases of Amah's beauty, of her father's wealth and wisdom, of his own nephew's fine prospects in the brick business. When at last he spelled out the marriage proposal and presented the bottle of gin, even old Boa could not restrain an appreciative "aah."

Aka knew that Boa would not give his answer right away. He would need about a month to consult all the members of his family and gain their approval of the marriage. Meanwhile, Aka could report that the visit had gone well.

On Aka's second visit to the family of Amah, it was Boa's turn to demonstrate his eloquence. He not only approved the marriage, he was "thunderstruck with joy" at the prospect of the union of the two families. He spoke of the Godlike dignity and honor of Aka and his kin and predicted that one day his village would boast skyscrapers built with Kassi's bricks.

"We will fix a date for the wedding," Boa announced, "and discuss the terms of the bride-price."

The "bride-price" is the payment which must be made to the bride's family for the bride. Among most other African groups, the bride-price discussion comes first, before the girl's family approves the marriage. It has become traditional for the Agni to pay only a small sum, usually no more than the equivalent of

❧ Boa predicted that one day his village would boast skyscrapers built with Kassi's bricks.

$10. But some Agni families still secretly agree to a much larger sum.

The Agni look upon a small payment as a symbol of goodwill and appreciation to the family of the bride. They believe that the payment of a large bride-price can trap a girl in an unwanted marriage. Her family will be reluctant to allow a divorce if the bride-price to be returned is too large. Besides, under the laws of the Ivory Coast, large bride-prices are forbidden.

Since Kassi had prospects of becoming very rich, Boa demanded a bride-price of about $400, much higher than usual. Kassi's family was stunned at this demand, but reluctantly agreed. The two families then agreed that the wedding should take place in one month. Kassi spent most of this time scraping together the bride-price money. By working at night, he doubled his brick production. He borrowed small sums from uncles, aunts, and cousins. His father donated three cows.

The bride-price was not Kassi's only marriage expense. He was expected to give presents to Amah, and money or liquor to her close relatives. And there was the traditional salt — a sack of it to be distributed to the old women of Amah's village. Only twice during this month could Kassi find the time to spend a few secret hours with Amah.

The wedding ritual was quick and businesslike. One of Boa's brothers took Amah's hand and spoke directly to Uncle Aka while Kassi stood by.

"I give you my niece's hand," Boa's brother said

loudly, "but first I must warn you about her bad character. She is lazy, a sly liar, and a thief." He went on to name all the evil habits he could think of. The purpose of this warning was to give the groom's family no cause to complain after the marriage. It was done solemnly, but Amah and Kassi could not help but smile at each other.

"I accept her in spite of these faults," Uncle Aka replied. This sealed the marriage, and the two families began a happy celebration which lasted far into the night.

Kassi's brick business prospered in the months that followed their marriage. New lumbering concerns and coffee plantations drew workers and their families to the village. The government was building a school nearby. Kassi sold his bricks as fast as he could form them. He repaid his debts and bought Amah all the dresses and market delicacies she wished. Yet a cloud began to gather over their marriage. A visit from Amah's mother finally brought the difficulty out into the open.

"Your father grows old," Amah's mother said to her. "He looks with envy at his friends who have grandchildren to play with. It is six months now, and you have no belly. Old Boa is ashamed."

"My time will come," Amah answered. "Tell my father he will have a grandson within a year." When her mother left, Amah discussed the matter with Kassi. They agreed to seek help.

The following week the couple consulted a doctor in Amah's village. The doctor gave them potions to take and advised them to sacrifice a goat. But as the months went by, they saw that there had been no cure. The prescriptions of other doctors proved no better.

☆ ☆ ☆ ☆ ☆ ☆ ☆ ☆ ☆

"We were married according to Agni custom," replied Kassi. "It is the law of the village and forest that will settle this matter."

A year passed. Now there was nagging from both their parents and the unspoken scorn of their friends. It was natural for Amah and Kassi each to believe that the other was at fault. Often minor disagreements led to angry, senseless accusations. One day, when Kassi complained that his dinner of fish and yams was burned, his wife turned on him.

"If you were a whole man," she cried, "I would cook you proper food." Enraged, Kassi threw the bowl at her and left the house. When he returned, he found that Amah had gone.

The next day, Amah's father came to Kassi's house.

"My daughter will never again sleep in this house," Boa snapped. "This fruitless marriage has brought shame to my family."

"And shame to mine," Kassi answered. "I will be pleased to be rid of this barren woman. Return the bride-price and we will divorce."

"No. It is wrong. There will be a divorce, yes. But the money was a mere symbol. You know I am not obliged to return it."

"Your daughter has given me no children," Kassi said angrily, "and she has abandoned my house. The money must be returned. Under the law."

The Nigerian couple at left in this photo have reached the end of an unhappy marriage. Since they were wed by a government official, they must be divorced in a court of law. The man holding the book is testifying in the husband's behalf.

86

"It is you who cannot make children. Besides, you are foolish to speak of law," Boa said. "Under the law, you are not even married."

Boa was speaking of the legal code of the Ivory Coast. Under the code, marriages are not official unless they are performed before a special government representative. In the interior, most villagers marry first according to their local customs. Then, sometimes years later, husband and wife will travel to the nearest large town where they formalize their marriage before an official. It was true that Kassi and Amah had not done this.

"We were married according to Agni custom," replied Kassi. "That is law enough. You speak of the laws of the city shops and factories. It is the law of the village and forest that will settle this matter." By "the law of the village and forest," Kassi meant individual local custom rather than any formal legal code.

The settlement of the divorce was a fairly simple matter. Boa knew that Kassi could not bring the dispute before an official court because the marriage was not valid under the legal code. Boa could bring it before the village chiefs, but he didn't want to do this either, since he knew these respected men would consider him greedy. He made up his mind to return some of the bride-price and agreed to let Mosu,* a respected elder of another village, decide how much.

The families came together on neutral ground in Mosu's village. Amah's relatives told how the bride-price payment was only a symbol and that what was returned should also be a symbol, only much smaller. Old Boa stood up himself and claimed he could raise only about $100. Uncle Aka answered by telling a fable about a sheep that had eaten the cub of a leopard.

"The sheep asked his friend the bird to hide him

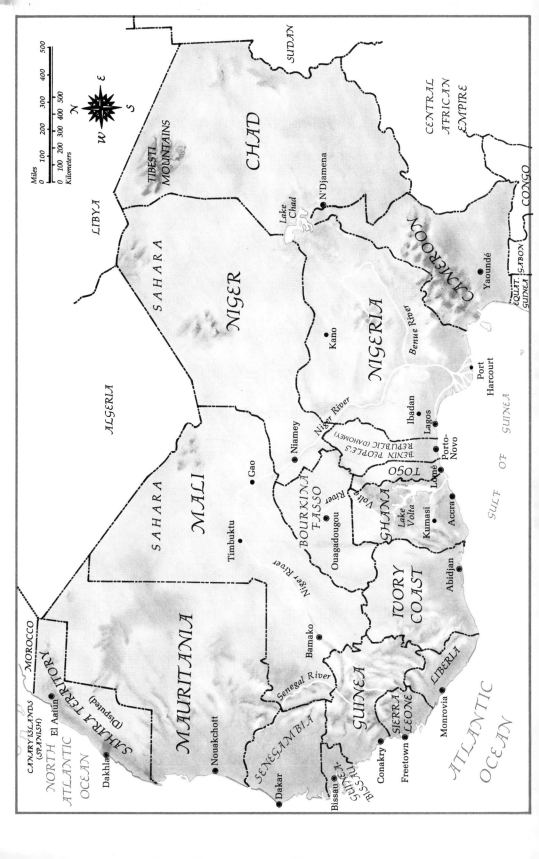

from the leopard's anger. So the bird tried to bury him. But it was a small bird, and it didn't dig deep enough. One of the sheep's legs stuck out above the ground. The leopard tripped over it, found the sheep, and killed him."

When Aka had finished, Kassi asked him why he had told the story.

"Like the sheep, Boa cannot conceal everything," Aka said triumphantly. "Today I learned from a friend that Boa has $200 set aside to buy land for coffee. This should be returned to us along with his $100. Then we will be satisfied." Mosu prompted Boa until he agreed.

The next day, Amah returned to Kassi's house for the last time. She stood while Kassi passed a loop of string over her head. Then he broke the string and said:

"Amah is no longer my wife."

Double-check

Review

1. Why was the festival of the yams a happy time in Kassi's Ivory Coast village?

2. Between whom do most African marriages represent an agreement?

3. Why would it take about a month for Boa to give his consent to his daughter's marriage?

4. What is a bride-price?

5. What did Kassi do to symbolize his divorce from Amah?

Discussion

1. What celebrations similar to the festival of the yams are there in your community? What purposes are served by such activities?

2. How do the engagement, wedding, and divorce rituals in Kassi's village differ from those in your community? In what ways are the African rituals similar to those with which you are most familiar?

3. Why was childbearing by married couples so important in Kassi and Amah's community? Do you think it is equally important in all African communities? Should couples who cannot have children be divorced? Why, or why not? Who should decide?

Activities

1. Some students might research and report on wedding customs of many countries, including their own. For example, they might find out why rice is thrown at weddings, where and why the traditional white bridal gown was first worn, and why fathers "give away" their daughters.

2. Some students might role-play the divorce settlement meeting of Amah and Kassi. Students could portray the young couple, their relatives, and elders who decide how much — if any — of the bride-price should be returned.

3. After some students report on marriage customs in various countries, others might research and report on divorce laws and practices.

Skills

LIFE EXPECTANCY

IN SOME WEST AFRICAN NATIONS

1980-1985

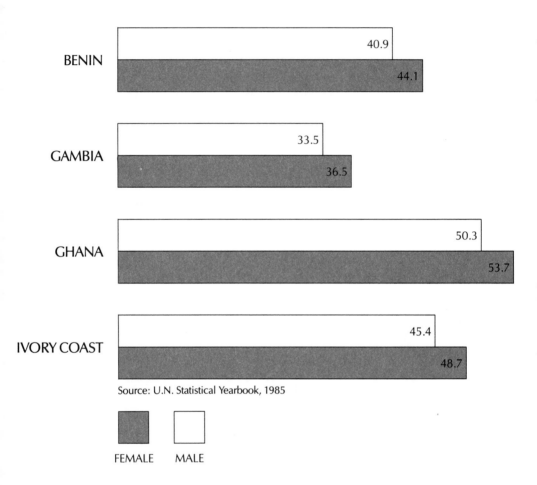

Source: U.N. Statistical Yearbook, 1985

FEMALE   MALE

Use the graph above and information in Chapter 6 to answer the following questions.

1. How many countries are represented in this graph?

2. In which country was the life expectancy for males the longest?

3. Who would be most likely to live longer, a male born on the Ivory Coast or a female born in Benin?

4. If Kassi and Amah had a daughter in 1985, how long would she have been expected to live?

Chapter 7

A Hunt for Food

IT WAS THE SECOND NIGHT without meat, and there was no dancing among the Bambuti* Pygmies. The women sat quietly in the doorways of their leaf-covered huts. Most of the men, including Sindula,* were gathered around the central fire. The flames burned low, barely lighting the men's faces and deepening the black of Zaïre's great Ituri Forest around them.

"It is a bad camp," one man said. "There are only leaves to eat here. We should move west." A few of the men murmured, agreeing with the suggestion.

"It is your aim that's bad," answered another. "And your net is weak. It is not the fault of the camp. The forest gave us a fine pig. Why did you give it back?" The teasing was good-natured and all the men laughed. But the talk of the pig only sharpened their hunger.

**≈§ The people in the camp took up
the song and sent it echoing out through
the blackness. They wanted to be sure
that the forest knew where they were so
that it could help them with the hunt.**

It had been a large old boar, suddenly awakened
by the noise of the hunt. He had been easily driven
into the hidden nets; but before any man could spear
him, he had slashed and torn his way out again with
his tusks. Instead of an excellent meal, enough for all
30 Pygmies in the camp, there was only a net to be
mended.

The men continued to joke with one another, and
gradually they forgot their growling stomachs. Some
lit clay pipes and puffed at them through long stems
cut from banana stalks. A few began to tell tales of
past hunts. They bragged of how hard they threw
their spears and how straight their poison-tipped arrows flew.

Sitting behind the other men, young Sindula listened to the stories. He wished he had a story of his
own to tell. But it was just a short time ago that his
mother had finished making his hunting net and he
had begun to cast with the men. There were still no
bloodstains on his net where an animal had been
caught and speared. Hunting alone with his bow and
arrows, Sindula had shot many birds and monkeys.
But these were not important enough to tell about at
the campfire.

"Tell about the elephant," someone said to one of
the older men. Others joined in: "The elephant. The
killing of the giant."

It was their favorite story — about a hunt many
years ago when two men alone had killed a bull ele-

phant. When the old hunter began his tale, the Pygmies moved closer to hear and see better. As he described the adventure, he acted out the most important parts: the great upward thrusts of the spears into the elephant's belly; the hunter hanging from a spear-handle to keep from being trampled; the agony of the huge beast; and, at last, the dividing of the mountain of meat. The Pygmies chuckled and gasped as the story unfolded.

When it was done, the old man sat down exhausted and, for a moment, the camp was quiet. Then, in the deep shadows on the edge of the clearing, a woman began to sing. The rest of the camp took up the song and sent it echoing out through the blackness around them. They wanted to be sure the forest knew where they were so that it could help them with the hunt the next day.

In the song, the Pygmies praised the kindness and beauty of the forest. They also sang of the food the forest gave them; of the tall trees and heavy leaves that sheltered and protected them; and of how thankful they were for fire which cheered and warmed them, and cooked their food. Some of the men and women were still singing several hours later when Sindula crept sleepily away to his hut.

A light rain fell during the night. The mongongo* leaves shingling Sindula's hut kept him dry. He slept well, scarcely stirring when an animal called or screamed from the forest. Awakening just before daybreak, he lay back contentedly on his bed of leaves and listened to the sounds of the camp preparing for the day.

After a few minutes, Sindula crawled out of his hut and went to bathe in the crystal stream just below the camp. He took off the small loincloth, the only garment Pygmy men and women wear, and slipped

into the cool water. Standing waist-deep, he splashed his face and neck clean. With a cry of delight, he pounced on a frog scrambling out on the far bank. Roasted on a green stick, it would make a delicious breakfast.

Sindula shared the frog with his mother and nibbled at a wild potato. His mind was on the hunt. He sat down on his hunting net and sharpened his spear, although it was already as fine as a razor.

Then the hunt began. The youngest of the men were sent out first. Five of them, including Sindula, headed west, the direction the camp elders had chosen the night before. Their bulky nets were slung over their shoulders and each carried a long-bladed spear. There were small knives tucked into the string belts of their loincloths. Sindula also took his bow and a quiver of poisoned arrows.

One of the youths carried a burning ember wrapped in several layers of leaves. This was to light a "hunting fire," which the Pygmies believed would help them in their hunt. Like the songs they had sung the night before, the fire was intended as a compliment to the forest and a reminder that they were hunting in that area and would welcome assistance.

The fire was kindled with leaves and twigs around a young tree. As it blazed higher, the other members of the hunt began to arrive. As they passed the hunting fire, each paused a moment in tribute to the forest. Then they scampered off down the narrow trail, chatting, laughing, whooping, and yelling.

After several hours, the noisy procession came to a halt. The group was on the edge of a valley through which a small river flowed. The lead hunters had de-

At the end of a successful hunt,
the men of a Pygmy village gather
to talk and sing far into the night.

*Carrying nets meant to trap their evening
meal, Pygmy men head out for another hunt.*

The youngest men went out first. They headed west, the direction the elders had chosen, their bulky nets slung over their shoulders.

cided to cast their nets here, using the river as a barrier that would keep animals from escaping around one side of their nets.

Now the laughing and shouting stopped. Only the noises of the forest could be heard. The men crept ahead for a quarter of a mile or so, then fanned out to place their nets. Some of the nets were nearly 300 feet long. When seven or eight of them were joined together, they formed a trap which would reach in an arc all the way up the side of the valley.

According to custom, the older and more experienced hunters placed their nets in the middle, the most likely place for game to be snared. Since Sindula was just a beginner at hunting, he was placed on the left end of the line of nets. Today this meant that his net would start at the river. It was a good place, and some of the older men thought Sindula was too young for such a spot, that his spear would miss. Sindula paid no attention and started down into the valley.

He fastened the end of his net to a sapling hanging over the river's edge. The bottom of the net he tied close to the ground and the top about four feet up the tree. He strung it out in this way for its full length of 150 feet, forming a four-foot-high fence of cords. Then he fastened the other end of his net to his neighbor's. As he worked he heard the other Pygmies "talking" back and forth by imitating the calls of birds and animals.

When his net was securely tied, and camouflaged as well as possible, Sindula stood back a short distance behind it, holding his spear. A few minutes later, he heard the tumultuous noise of the women beaters, the noise that would drive the animals into the trap. They shrieked, whistled, clapped, and whooped as they tramped through the trees. Sindula grinned and tightened his grip on the spear.

From the pitch of the women's cries, Sindula could tell what kind of game was being flushed. He knew that there was a large antelope near the top of the valley and several boloki* antelopes down below. He had seen one of these, but the tiny boloki had seen him too and scooted off along the line of nets. Sindula heard the shouting as the boloki was speared several hundred yards away. As the women closed in toward the nets, Sindula began to believe that he would return to camp again with nothing to show for the hunt.

There was a lull in the shouting up the hill. A faint sound of splashing reached Sindula's ears. He crouched and noiselessly made his way down to the river. Holding onto the tree where he had fastened the end of his net, he leaned out over the water just in time to see a large okapi* climb out on the far shore.

Sindula rushed back to the spot where he had left his bow and arrows. But he wasn't quick enough. By the time he returned, the okapi was swallowed up by the dense undergrowth along the riverbank.

For Sindula, the prize of the okapi was too great to lose. He slipped into the river, holding his arrows above his head where the water couldn't wash away their sticky brown poison. Quietly he paddled across.

Okapis are found only in the Ituri Forest and are extremely rare even there. Sindula had seen only one other before this. Its forelegs and hindquarters were striped black and white, and its head and long neck looked half giraffe and half antelope. It stood more than five feet tall at the shoulder.

⊸ᶳ Suddenly, there was a crunching sound from the left of the clearing. Slowly, slowly, Sindula fitted an arrow onto his bowstring and leaned forward.

"A feast," Sindula said to himself. His stomach squeezed tight as he thought how the camp would celebrate. Sliding out on the bank, he quickly located the okapi's footprints in the mud. An animal trail led into the forest.

The underbrush was much thicker on this side of the river. The trail was a dark, narrow tunnel through the dense foliage. Occasionally Sindula saw freshly broken twigs, water droplets, and other signs that the okapi had passed.

With no wind to carry Sindula's scent ahead, he moved along as quickly as he could. His feet glided over the forest floor without a sound. Suddenly he rounded a bend in the trail and stopped short. An explosion of light just ahead dazzled him. It was a clearing, an opening to the sun. Sindula dropped to his knees and squinted, trying to see if what he sensed was correct — that the okapi had stopped and was watching the clearing. Motionless, Sindula concentrated all his senses into his eyes and ears. He saw birds and butterflies swoop and flutter in the glitter of the clearing. And, from far behind him, he heard the voices of the other hunters.

"Where is our young hunter?" they said. "Is his net so bloody that he has to rest somewhere? Or is he hunting animals that he can catch more easily, like termites?"

"Don't follow my trail," thought Sindula. "Or I'll never kill this animal."

The shouting soon faded away, leaving only the or-

❧ Sindula felt no sympathy for the suffering animal. He considered it as just so much meat.

dinary sounds of the forest. There were birdcalls, the grunting of a pig, the soft buzz of bees. "Honey," Sindula said to himself, relaxing a bit. "Soon it will be the season for honey again."

Suddenly there was a crunching sound from just to the left of the clearing. Slowly, slowly, Sindula fitted an arrow onto his bowstring and leaned forward. The okapi was there!

Sensing danger, it moved about uncertainly, sniffing high in the air. Then, seeming to make up its mind, it loped along the edge of the clearing, heading for the trail that continued into the forest opposite where Sindula waited.

The shot was an easy one. The arrow hit several inches below the shoulder, near the heart, where the poison would work quickly. Sindula was overjoyed. He leaped into the clearing, not even thinking to try to get another shot before the animal galloped off down the trail.

"Okapi," cried Sindula. "I have killed the okapi." He yelled partly for joy and partly to summon the other Pygmies who would have to help carry the meat back to camp. "Okapeee-eeee," he yelled again until at last there was an answering cry from back toward the river. Then he broke off a branch, placed it in the clearing as a sign to the others, and ran after the animal.

Again the trail was a dark tunnel, but the spatterings of blood were clearly visible. They became more and more frequent as the animal slowed. Then they stopped entirely, and Sindula could see where the okapi had broken into the underbrush on one side. He found it lying a few yards away.

"Okapi," Sindula cried again. He danced around the animal as it tried to fight its way to its feet. Sindula felt no sympathy for the suffering animal. He considered it as just so much meat. Just before the okapi died, Sindula took his knife and cut away the flesh around the arrow wound. The poison was concentrated there, and that meat would not be safe to eat. Then he sat down on the animal and waited.

Scarcely five minutes passed before Sindula heard excited chatter and feet pounding down the trail toward him.

"Okapeeee-eeee," he called, laughing aloud. "Here. Here." Two of the younger men crashed through the underbrush. Others followed — even a few of the women — all who could swim the river. They poked and prodded the okapi and warmly praised Sindula and his hunting skill.

The carcass was far too heavy to carry whole back to camp, so it was decided to divide the meat there. According to custom, Sindula and the older hunters got the choicest pieces. Then Sindula tried to divide the meat fairly among the others.

"The forelegs to the two swift men who arrived here first," he began. "The head to the wise man who chose this valley for the hunt." But it was no use. The others knew just how much meat they were entitled to. Laughing, they hacked and grabbed until all the okapi was gone. The march back to camp began. Tired as they were, and in spite of the cargo of meat they carried, the Pygmies shouted and ran the entire distance.

The celebration that night was even finer than Sindula had imagined it would be. The Pygmies stuffed themselves with meat. When they were done, there

Most Pygmy villages consist of a cluster of
leafy huts encircled in a cathedral of trees.
At the center of the village clearing stand the
drums used to summon the spirits of the forest.

was still plenty left for the next day. Men and women
dressed up, sticking leaves in their beltstrings and
feathers in their hair. Some of the girls fingerpainted
themselves with bright-colored dyes. All danced and
sang, and the men made music with tom-toms and
reed pipes and plucked on their bowstrings.

Sindula acted out the hunt three times and each
time he did it better. He fought the swift current of
the river, he sped like an antelope down the dark jungle trail, he tricked the shrewd okapi into showing

himself, he shot his arrow like a streak of lightning. The spectators laughed and clapped louder and louder.

It was almost morning when Sindula left the central fire. There had been a thousand songs about this hunt and ones past, about the forest and its great gift of the okapi. But the singing had gradually died as Pygmy families crept away into their huts.

Sindula still didn't feel like sleep. There was too much joy left in his heart. Instead, he climbed into a mahogany tree that reached over the camp. Grabbing a vine, he swung out over the roofs of the huts below.

"Okapeee-eeee," he yelled. "Okapeeeeeeee."

Double-check

Review

1. In what country is the Ituri Forest?

2. Why did the Pygmies sing in the forest at night?

3. Why did Sindula place his net at the end of the line of hunters?

4. Why did the women whistle and clap as they tramped through the forest?

5. Why did Sindula kill the okapi?

Discussion

1. What are some practical reasons for the Pygmies to hunt together instead of individually? Do you think group hunting is done only for practical reasons? What might be some other reasons and benefits to the group that account for group hunting?

2. In what ways does this chapter show the respect Pygmies have for the older members of their community? How are older people shown respect in your community?

3. What social purposes, other than mere bragging, are served by the telling and retelling of hunting stories? Could such stories have been the breeding grounds for rituals, drama, and literature? How?

Activities

1. Some students (or the whole class) might take a trip to a nearby zoo or museum to look at examples of African animals. Other students might prepare a bulletin board display of photos and pictures from old magazines showing African animals, especially those common to Zaïre and the Ituri Forest.

2. A skilled and experienced hunter might be invited to speak to the class about reasons and techniques for group hunting. This speaker might also be invited to take part in a discussion of the arguments for and against hunting for nonsurvival purposes.

3. Some students might research and report on the changing lives of the remaining Pygmy tribes in Africa. Others might report on Pygmies in other parts of the world.

Skills

HUNTERS AND GATHERERS

Hunters and gatherers . . . are very much part of the land that sustains them. To survive they must be in balance with what the land can offer them. They have a faith in the resources of their physical world, and in their own ability to exploit them. They live in small, intimate, cooperating bands as part of a diverse but familiar tribe, moving nomadically from camp to camp as food resources or their own whim may dictate. Hoarding material possessions is foreign to them, but this does not prevent them developing a rich culture and elaborate ritual. . . .

— Richard E. Leakey and Roger Lewin,
Origins (New York: E.P. Dutton, 1977)

Use the passage above and information in Chapter 7 to answer the following questions.

1. In the passage above, the word *they* refers to what group of people?
(a) familiar tribes   (b) farmers   (c) hunters and gatherers

2. Nomadic people live where?
(a) in rich cities   (b) in temporary camps   (c) on farms

3. *Hoarding material possessions* means what in this passage?
(a) buying valuable objects
(b) collecting things
(c) developing a rich culture

4. From reading this passage, one can conclude that hunters and gatherers do what for a living?
(a) work for farmers   (b) live off the land   (c) develop a rich culture

5. Which of the following is probably true about Sindula?
(a) He lives in the same camp all year.
(b) He collects valuable things.
(c) He moves a lot.

3
THE
AFRICAN
ECONOMY

Chapter 8

Land and Livelihood

NOT LONG AGO a villager in the African nation of Zambia* wrote to a local newspaper asking for some advice. He lived near a bus stop, he explained, and many friends and relatives from his home village, which he had left a few years before, stopped off to visit while going to and from the capital of Lusaka.* "According to custom, it is my duty to give my tribesfolk food and money for their journey," he wrote. "But I am kept poor by these people, even though I have a good job. I do not dislike them, but what can I do to be saved from them?"

The question was a deadly serious one. Among Africans still bound by family and community ties, unwanted guests are no laughing matter. If such guests come often enough or stay long enough, they can eat their host almost out of house and home. He may be forced to choose between the older values such as family loyalty and the demands of personal well-being forced by a new, changing Africa.

Like the man with the unwanted guests, Africans often find themselves faced with conflicts between older and newer ways of doing things. Such conflicts not only affect ways of spending money; they also affect ways of making it.

Most Africans rely on the land around them for a living. For centuries, almost all Africans were farmers or hunters. Now many work in industry and commerce, but most still farm or hunt. In Tropical Africa three out of every four people earn their livelihood in this way today. Compared with people in other parts of the world, that is a high percentage indeed.

Africans who live off the land fall into three main groups. They are:

Hunters and food gatherers. Today very few Africans make their living simply by hunting wild animals or plucking wild fruit and berries. Of the people who do, the two best-known groups are the Pygmies (see Chapter 7) and the San (see pages 26-28).

The San people, who are sometimes called Bushmen, live in caves or small huts on the Kalahari Desert of South-West Africa and Botswana.* They seek out their quarry — antelopes, for example — by following footprints in the sand. Often they kill the animal with arrows dipped in poison. Then they carry the carcass back to camp where they skin and butcher it for meat.

Herdsmen. As their name implies, these people make their living mainly by raising cows, sheep, and goats. Whereas hunters move about in search of animals, herdsmen often wander in search of grazing lands for their herds. Nowadays few of these people limit themselves solely to raising livestock. Many have settled in villages where they grow food crops.

◄§ **African cattlemen rarely raise their cows for slaughter. Instead, they keep them for the milk they produce.**

With his bow and his spear held in readiness, a Masai herdsman of East Africa keeps careful watch while his cattle take an afternoon drink.

African cattlemen rarely raise their cows for slaughter. Instead they keep their cows for the milk they produce. Above all, Africans prize cattle as a sign of wealth and prestige.

Farmers. Farmers make up the vast majority of Africa's villagers. Many of these people also herd cows and goats and sheep in addition to cultivating the soil. Yet it is virtually impossible to single out any of these millions of people as being typical of the rest. Part of the reason is that African farmers, like all Africans, are caught up in many changes. And change affects different farmers in very different ways.

As a case in point, consider the most traditional of these people — the so-called subsistence* farmer. A subsistence farmer grows only enough food to feed the family, with little or nothing left over to take to market. Chances are that he or she works land owned by a family group or an entire village rather than by any single individual. And chances are that the farmer plants and harvests according to ancient rules.

It's likely, for example, that the land is cleared by a method known as "slash and burn." Generally speaking, "slash-and-burn" farming works like this: Each year before the rains come, farmers hack down trees and brush, and set fire to them. Removing the brush prepares the land for cultivation. Ashes from the debris provide a fertilizer to nourish the farmers' crops. The great benefit of subsistence farming is that it is straightforward. Dinner grows in gardens just beyond a farmer's own front door.

What food the farmer does not grow is usually obtained through barter. Kenya's first president, Jomo Kenyatta,* explained barter this way:

"If one man has beans and another yams, he goes to a man who has yams and wants beans and tells him, 'I have my beans and I want your yams.' Then they argue

112

as to how many yams a basket of beans. If they agree, they exchange there and then; if not, each goes his own way, looking for someone else who will agree with him."

The subsistence farmer has been a mainstay of the African social order for centuries. Even so, his way of life has some built-in drawbacks. One of them is that such farming restricts the foods a family eats to items which the farmer raises *himself* or obtains through barter. As a result, farm families often get too much of one kind of food and not enough of another.

The food they eat least is meat. Without meat, many Africans fail to get enough protein, which is essential to good health. When children do not get enough protein, they sometimes develop a disease known as *kwashiorkor**. In severe cases this disease can cause crippling or even death.

Usually, however, malnutrition does not kill quickly. The drought of 1979-1984 has exhibited this. Little or no rain fell on areas of Ethiopia, Chad, the Sudan, Mali, and Niger. Even prosperous farmers soon had no food at all. Eventually they became refugees—desperate people searching for food and water. Hundreds of thousands of Africans have slowly died of starvation and disease.

The United States and other Western nations have tried to end the suffering and hunger. They have sent thousands of tons of grain and other supplies to the stricken nations. An estimated three million lives have been saved. But simply shipping food is not enough. Many of the famine areas are hemmed in by mountains. Often it is almost impossible to get food and supplies to starving people. In addition, the governments of some African nations have done little to help famine victims. Sometimes they even make it difficult for other nations to help. The Ethiopian government is a prime example of this. Ethiopian soldiers hinder food ship-

ments to stricken areas in the north, because they oppose the revolutionaries who live there. The government has made matters even worse by levying a $1 million port tax on a shipload of food and supplies sent by Westerners.

Even after victims of famine are saved from starvation, they will suffer long-term problems. Children's minds and bodies are stunted from the effects of slow starvation. Some go blind from vitamin A deficiency. Older children fail to mature. Babies have abnormally low birth weights.

Recently, there has been increased hope for the starving in Africa. The Live Aid/Band Aid rock concerts of 1985 raised over $50 million for trucks and supplies. In addition, the African grain harvests of 1985 were the best in years, due to increased rainfall and shipments of seed, fertilizer, and tools. The United Nations estimated that the number of hungry people would drop from 27 million to 19 million in 1986. With adequate rainfall and continued aid, the crisis might soon be over.

Two other factors could help end famine for good in Africa. Firstly, the African peoples could try to end overpopulation, which is a primary cause of famine. Secondly, improved farming methods could produce more food.

Most African governments have already begun programs to help farmers grow more food. They encourage people to pool their land and resources so they can buy tractors and make money from the five main cash crops—cocoa, cotton, coffee, peanuts, and palm oil. With money, farmers are able to buy a wider variety of foods. Potentially, this could put a stop to poverty and malnutrition. It has already enabled many African farmers to live by their profits where they once lived only by their wits.

What does this photo of workers stacking peanuts have to do with "cash-crop" farming?

115

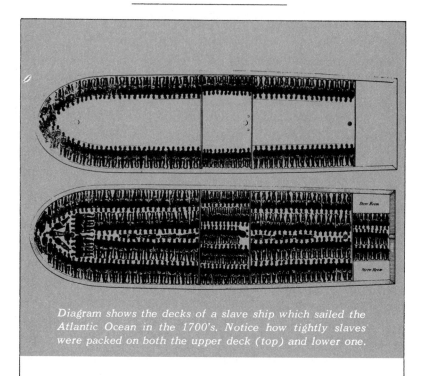

Diagram shows the decks of a slave ship which sailed the Atlantic Ocean in the 1700's. Notice how tightly slaves were packed on both the upper deck (top) and lower one.

JOURNEY INTO DESPAIR

THE FIRST THING Olaudah Equiano* noticed as he approached the sea was a slave ship lying at anchor along the coast. Before he knew it, he had been carried on board the ship and inspected by its crew.

"I now saw myself deprived of all chance of returning to my native country," he wrote many years later. "I was soon put down under the decks, and there I received such a salutation [greeting] in my nostrils as I had never experienced in my life.... I became so sick and low that I was not able to eat, nor had I the least desire to taste anything. I now wished for death."

The year was 1755, and 10-year-old Olaudah Equiano was a slave bound from what is now Nigeria to the island of Barbados* in the far-off Caribbean Sea. He was not the first African to be shipped into slavery, and he would not be the last. Yet Equiano's description of his voyage has echoed down the centuries. For it expressed the despair felt by millions of African slaves as they made similar journeys over a period of more than 400 years.

Equiano's journey would have a happy ending. In time he would learn to read and write, and manage to buy his own freedom. But this was an exception to one of the cruelest tales ever to unfold: the African slave trade. It is a story of wars and kidnappings, suffering and death.

Historians do not know exactly when or where African slavery began. But they believe it grew out of the need of certain African groups to enforce their own laws. Sometime in the now-forgotten past, these groups began making slaves of criminals, troublemakers, and prisoners of war. In some cases slaves were put to work by those who enslaved them. In other cases they were sold to distant groups. Whatever their fate, few of them were held in bondage for a lifetime. Sooner or later most were set free.

This form of slavery continued for hundreds, perhaps thousands, of years without much interference from the outside world. Then, in the 11th century, Arab merchants began pressing south of the Sahara in search of markets for their goods. In the course of their trade, the Arabs purchased some black Africans, making them slaves for life.

It wasn't until the 15th century that Europeans took an active part in slave trade. The first people to do so were the Portuguese — and they stumbled into it almost by accident. In the early 1400's, Portuguese sailors began sailing southward along the West African coast in order to tap the ancient trade in gold. By 1441 these seamen had journeyed to the northern edge of Tropical Africa and brought back a dozen slaves.

Their human cargo was the first trickle in what would soon become a swollen stream. But in 1441 Europeans

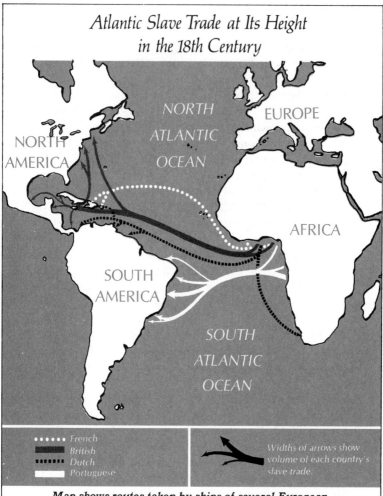

Atlantic Slave Trade at Its Height in the 18th Century

NORTH ATLANTIC OCEAN

EUROPE

NORTH AMERICA

AFRICA

SOUTH AMERICA

SOUTH ATLANTIC OCEAN

••••• French
▬▬▬ British
▪▪▪▪▪ Dutch
▬▬▬ Portuguese

Widths of arrows show volume of each country's slave trade.

Map shows routes taken by ships of several European countries in sending slaves from Africa to the Americas.

had little need for slaves. The demand was not created until 1492. In that year Christopher Columbus sailed west from Palos,* Spain, and sighted land in the Americas. Back in Europe reports of his adventures touched off a race to open up two continents.

Suddenly vast numbers of men were wanted in the Americas to chop down forests, till the soil, and build towns. Since European settlers in the New World couldn't fill the need for laborers, they turned to Africa for help. By the middle of the 16th century, Portuguese merchants had become veterans at the African trade. And so, at about this time, Spain began asking Portugal to supply Spanish colonies in America with black slaves.

All the while, Europeans had been building trading stations, known as "factories," up and down a long section of the West African coast. There they carried on a growing exchange of goods for slaves. The trade often went something like this: Africans living along the coast would go inland and obtain slaves either by trade or kidnapping or war. Then these African traders would bring their captives back to the factories and sell them to European traders.

Black people sold into bondage came from nearly every part of Africa and from a variety of groups. Their enslavement stripped them of almost everything they had once held dear — their families and their neighbors, their religion, and their pride. Few of them would ever regain their freedom. Instead they were packed aboard slave ships and sent off to become strangers in some strange new land.

This journey was known as "Middle Passage." At best it was heartbreaking, and often it was far, far worse. Men, women, and children were stuffed onto ships so crowded that there was barely room to sit or stand. When diseases struck, they spread swiftly, sometimes taking scores of lives in a single day. By some estimates no more than one in four enslaved Africans actually reached the New World. Others guess that figure may be one in two. No one knows — or ever will.

The people who profited from this grisly business were scattered across four continents. They included Africans who sold slaves, Europeans who kidnapped and transported them, and landowners in North and South America who bought the slaves and worked them. Because the slave trade reaped large profits, the Portuguese were soon unable to keep it to themselves. In the 17th century, Britain, France, and the Netherlands took a piece of the market. Soon almost every seafaring nation in Europe had also become involved.

Slave trading hit its peak between 1720 and 1820, as thousands upon thousands of black people were chained together and made to sail the seas. Yet even as this traffic crested, slavery became the object of harsher and harsher criticism. Europe's economic fortunes were improving, and slavery was coming to seem more and more outdated. What was equally important, it was coming to seem needlessly, senselessly cruel.

Religious groups such as the Quakers and the Methodists denounced it. So did many Europeans belonging to no religious sect at all. As such criticism grew louder and the slave trade became less necessary, Britain did away with slavery in the home islands in 1772. Early in the 1800's, Britain, Denmark, and the U.S. banned the international trade in slaves.

But it was one thing to outlaw the slave trade, and another thing to end it. For many years after this traffic had become illegal, the demand for slaves continued — especially in Cuba and Brazil. Smugglers built small fortunes by meeting this demand illegally. And with the increase in smuggling, conditions aboard slave ships grew steadily worse.

Finally, Britain cracked down. It stationed a mighty naval force in the Atlantic Ocean to drive slave ships from the seas. It also persuaded the Spanish and the Brazilians to enforce their own laws much more strictly. In the 1860's, the Atlantic slave traffic began to dwindle. The Arabs continued such trade in East Africa on a small scale. But by 1890 the ugly trade in humans had nearly disappeared.

It was gone but not forgotten. How could it be forgotten when it had so great an impact on the settlement of two continents? Today the North and South American population includes an estimated 50 to 60 million people of African or partly African descent. Theirs is a proud heritage. But their journey to the New World is a shameful reminder of how greed brought about man's cruelest inhumanity to man.

Double-check

Review

1. Africans who live off the land fall into what three main groups?

2. What is one drawback of subsistence farming?

3. In what two ways have most African governments fought malnutrition?

4. What are the five most important cash crops in Tropical Africa?

5. What groups of people profited from the African slave trade?

Discussion

1. If you moved to Africa and intended to live off the land, which would you rather be — farmer, herdsman, or hunter and gatherer? Why?

2. The economies of many African nations depend on single crops. What are some advantages — and disadvantages — of single-crop economies? Should the governments of such nations try to change their economies? If so, how? What might they do to get farmers to plant other crops?

3. Do you think the story of African slave trade will ever be forgotten? Should it ever be forgotten? Why, or why not? What motivations, other than greed, might have caused people to take part in slave trade? Do such motivations still exist in the world today? Explain your answers.

Activities

1. Some students might role-play a meeting between government officials of an African nation and several subsistence farmers whom the officials are trying to persuade to pool their land for cash-crop farming. The farmers are suspicious of the change and worried about how they will get food to eat, but they are willing to listen to the government officials.

2. Some students might research and report answers to the following question: In what ways, if any, did the enslavement of Africans by Europeans differ from other forms of slavery in human history? The research might include an examination of slavery in the ancient Greek, Roman, and Egyptian empires.

3. Other students might read a few firsthand accounts by Africans who survived the Middle Passage. *Afro-American History: Primary Sources,* edited by Thomas Frazier (New York: Harcourt, Brace & World, 1970), contains autobiographical accounts by a prince, a Moslem, and other West Africans, including Olaudah Equiano.

Skills

MILK PRODUCTION, 1978

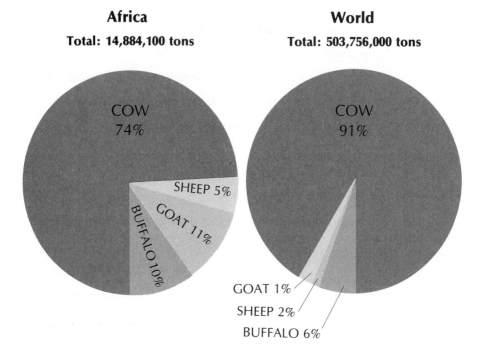

Africa	World
Total: 14,884,100 tons	**Total: 503,756,000 tons**

Source: *U.N. Statistical Yearbook, 1978*

Use the circle graphs above and information in Chapter 8 to answer the following questions.

1. What does the graph on the left show? What does the graph on the right show?

2. What fact about milk production is made clear by a quick glance at these graphs?

3. What animals account for a greater percentage of African milk production than of world milk production?

4. How many tons of milk were produced by goats throughout the world in 1978?

5. Which statements in Chapter 8 about African cattlemen seem to be proven true by one of the above graphs?

122

Chapter 9

A Scrap of Paper

EVER SINCE RETURNING to his homeland of Ghana, Akwasi Gambaga* had lived the life of a serious-minded young bachelor. He had rented an apartment on the northern fringe of the country's capital, Accra,* and traveled to and from his office by bicycle. As he pedaled his way down tree-lined boulevards and around public squares, he paid little attention to his surroundings. His mind was usually on his job.

Akwasi's job was with Ghana's Cocoa Council. This was the government agency which controlled the production and price of cocoa, the source of chocolate. He had applied for the job while he was studying to be a lawyer in faraway Britain. The salary was high, and he could use the experience with the marketing board to build a political career later.

Akwasi was well aware how important cocoa was to the life of his nation. Ghana was one of the world's leading producers of cocoa beans, its leading

In the tradition of college students everywhere, these African leaders-to-be are gathered in a rap session. The scene of their conference is a student lounge at the University of Nigeria.

crop. As a boy, Akwasi had watched his elders care for the cocoa trees and harvest their beans. He knew the routine as well as he knew his own name.

Cocoa farmers plant their trees in the protective shade of the forest. After four or five years, the slender white saplings begin to bear fruit. First, thousands of tiny pink flowers bloom on the trunk and main branches. About 20 of these later become the pods that hold seeds or cocoa beans.

The pods are shaped like footballs and are about eight inches long. When they turn from green to a golden color, cocoa growers slash them open and scoop out the pulp-covered beans. They pack the beans between layers of huge plantain* leaves. In a few days the sugary pulp around the beans ferments into a liquid and drains away. For the final step,

124

the beans are placed on mats to dry in the sun.

The Cocoa Council provides a sort of price insurance for the thousands of cocoa farmers in Ghana. Most of these farmers own only a few acres of cocoa trees, and they badly need protection against a possible sharp drop in the world price of their crop.

The price drop may occur in times of economic depression. Then cocoa is considered an expensive luxury, and fewer people will buy it. The price may also drop when good weather results in an exceptionally large crop and the supply of cocoa exceeds the demand. But whether the world price rises or falls, the government Cocoa Council pays Ghana's farmers a stable price. Thus farmers are always assured an income from their crop.

The council usually sells the cocoa for more than it pays the farmers for it. Some of this cash surplus is set aside against the possibility of a price drop. Some is spent on education and on research into better methods of farming cocoa and controlling the diseases that plague the trees.

As a lawyer, Akwasi worked with the council's legal department. In his first few months in the job, he spent most of his time brushing up his knowledge of laws dealing with cocoa farming. On week days he worked late at the office and frequently brought papers home to study at night. On free evenings he sometimes went to British or American movies, or went dancing with friends at one of Accra's night spots.

Many of Akwasi's friends worked for government agencies as he did. They were generally graduates of Ghana's universities, although a few of them had studied in Britain as Akwasi had. Akwasi found that he had to be careful with those who had not studied abroad. For if he acted too "British" with them, they felt that he was being a snob.

What puzzled Akwasi about this was that these same friends could be a little snobbish themselves. Akwasi sometimes rode his bike to nearby villages where he talked with people and took part in some of their activities. But none of his city friends would go with him on these trips. They looked down their noses at country people and made fun of those who still practiced "country" ways.

One of the people who most resented Akwasi's British education was his boss, Mr. Kobina.* Mr. Kobina had been educated at one of Ghana's lesser-known schools. He envied Akwasi and showed little interest in any new ideas that Akwasi proposed. Mr. Kobina was afraid of change.

In his first few weeks in the job, Akwasi noticed that Mr. Kobina got to work late, took an extra hour for lunch, and did little work even when he was at his desk. As a result, Akwasi lost respect for him. Mr. Kobina had gotten his job through a relative who was a government official. This way of selecting officials from one's family is becoming less common in Africa. But it is a natural result of the obligations that all Africans feel toward their relatives, even distant ones.

One afternoon in January Mr. Kobina called Akwasi into his office and waved a letter at him.

"It's the Ashanti* again. The Ashanti people are always causing trouble," said Mr. Kobina, who belonged to a different group. The letter was from an Ashanti chief who complained that the Cocoa Council had been paying too little for his people's cocoa.

Akwasi received permission to visit the chief and explain in person how the price had been determined. Mr. Kobina was happy to have him out of the office, and Akwasi welcomed the chance to get away. It was the middle of the dry season in Accra. The heat was uncomfortable, and the *harmattan*,* the dry wind

⇜ When cocoa pods turn from green to gold, growers slash them open and scoop out the beans.

Farmers remove cocoa beans from their pods.

that blows south from the Sahara, was covering the streets with dust. Perhaps it would be cooler in the shade of the forest.

A short train ride brought Akwasi to Kumasi,* the bustling capital of the Ashanti region. There Akwasi found a "Mammy Wagon" that would take him directly to the village of the chief. Mammy Wagons are usually small, rundown vehicles which chug back and forth from village to city, often bringing traders and their goods to market. The owners, usually women, dress up their trucks with slogans or comments chalked on the front and back. Many have religious meanings, but some are meant to be amusing. The Mammy Wagon which would take Akwasi into cocoa country was grimly lettered "The Last Ride."

Akwasi sat down on the wooden plank that served as a seat. As the wagon bumped along, he puzzled over what he would say. The Ashanti people have a long and proud history, and though their village chiefs have little national authority, they still expect to be treated with respect. Akwasi knew that his dealings with the chief would call for a great deal of tact.

When he arrived at the chief's village, Akwasi showed the letter to the first man he met. The man could not read, but he recognized his chief's seal and signature and immediately led Akwasi to the largest house in the village. Akwasi was soon led inside.

The chief's face and bearing were kingly. He was seated on a beautifully carved wooden stool, the traditional symbol of the Ashanti people. He wore a fur cap spangled with gold stars and was dressed in a gleaming robe of Kente* cloth, Ghana's world-famous fabric woven of silk and cotton. In his right hand, the chief held a cane to protect himself from evil. He looked straight at Akwasi.

Around the chief stood several of his attendants.

128

One carried a pair of talking drums with their special bent-tipped drumsticks. A second held a heavy scepter molded of silver. As the chief's spokesman, this man would be the one to talk with Akwasi, since an Ashanti chief traditionally does not speak directly to others.

The spokesman talked at length of the merit of the villagers' cocoa beans and how the chief knew that the government Cocoa Council would sell them for a higher price than it paid. Akwasi admitted this and explained the reasons why. It was a discussion that Akwasi had conducted many times before.

Suddenly the chief raised his hand to stop the talk and whispered a few Ashanti words. Much to Akwasi's surprise, all but the chief left the house. Now the chief asked Akwasi to sit down, and he began to talk.

"We are not as strongly bound by tradition as before," the chief said, "so I will speak to you directly concerning a matter which has been much on my mind. This is the real reason for my letter — I was hoping someone like you would come here. The problem is our inheritance laws. As you know, in our community a child belongs always to the clan of his mother. For many years this has created difficulties for cocoa growers. Can you help me find a solution?"

Akwasi was familiar with this problem, which plagues many of the Ashanti people. It stems from the Ashanti belief that a child receives his body and blood entirely from his mother. From his father he receives spiritual matter, important for those questions pertaining to after-life rather than those pertaining to the present. Thus, a child always belongs to the clan of his mother, not his father. This is known as matrilineal* descent.

Since Ashanti land must be kept within a clan, a father cannot will it to his sons, who are members of

their mother's clan. Instead, when the father dies, the land passes to the children of his sisters. Thus, a cocoa farm worked by an entire family over many years may be passed to a nephew who lives in another village.

"But this is clearly a matter of local custom," Akwasi answered the chief. "I am not even an Ashanti. How can I be of any help?"

"You are a lawyer. My village needs a new law. We have ceremonies now in which a father may give his cocoa trees, although not his land, to his sons. But for various reasons some do not perform this ceremony before they die. And then the ancient rules must be obeyed. A written law might help us to avoid this."

"But would your people obey this law? A scrap of paper written on by a man in a faraway city?"

"Write me the law, and we will see. It is a change that is needed. We welcome any change that will not disturb our ancestors, that will help the Ashantis and leave the soul of our people in peace."

Later, on the train taking him back to Accra, Akwasi thought over what the chief had said.

"If only all Ghanaians had the good sense of that Ashanti chief," he thought to himself. "He cherishes those traditions which are a source of strength for his people, and he tries to change useless customs which have now become harmful. I wish all our people could see our problems as clearly as he does."

An Ashanti chief greets his villagers. How does this photo show the sense of affection which exists between this leader and those he serves?

Double-check

Review

1. What is the Cocoa Council in Ghana?

2. What are two situations that could lead to a price drop in cocoa?

3. What was the traditional symbol of the Ashanti people?

4. Why did the Ashanti children belong always to the clan of their mothers?

5. What type of changes did the Ashanti chief welcome?

Discussion

1. The Ashanti chief had little authority outside of his village. Yet the national government treated him with respect. Why do you think the government did this?

2. Why do you think Akwasi's college-educated friends made fun of people who lived in villages instead of cities? Why didn't Akwasi look down on villagers? Do city people look down on country people in the United States? In your community?

3. Akwasi wanted a political career in the future. Do you think he would be a good governmental leader? Give reasons for your answer.

Activities

1. Some students might prepare a bulletin board entitled "Leading Crops of Africa." Use pictures cut from newspapers and magazines, or your own drawings, to illustrate the board. Pictures might be grouped according to the nations from which each crop comes.

2. A botanist might be invited to discuss with the class the types of crops that grow in Africa and the reasons why certain crops grow better in some geographic areas than in others.

3. The Ashanti chief has asked you, not Akwasi, to write a law allowing fathers to give their cocoa trees to their sons. Write the law in such a way that it would bring no offense to Ashanti ancestors, but would help the living villagers.

Skills

COCOA BEAN PRODUCTION, 1971-1981

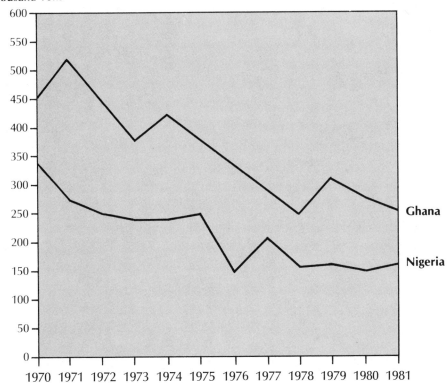

Thousand Tons

Source: U.N. Statistical Yearbook, 1982

Use the line graph above and information in Chapter 9 to answer the following questions.

1. What do the numbers in the vertical column on the left side of the graph represent? The numbers along the bottom?

2. What does a quick glance at the graph show about cocoa bean production between 1970 and 1981 in Ghana and Nigeria?

3. In what year was cocoa bean production in Ghana the greatest?

4. In what year was cocoa bean production in Ghana and Nigeria the farthest apart?

5. If all other things were normal, during which of the above years might there have been a drop in the price of Ghana's cocoa beans?

THE LAND

Out beyond its cities, Africa still
rings with the morning noises of a
partly untamed frontier. Waterfalls still
splash and gurgle along the Zambezi*
River. Zebras still rustle the golden
grass of the East African plain.

136

TERRAIN: Though much of the African landscape is flat and open, it also has its ups and downs. Top left, the majestic calm of Lesotho's Maluti Mountains. Left, the cool white tapestry of Tanzania's Mt. Kilimanjaro. Above, the roaring chasm of Victoria Falls.

LIVING SPACE: Nowadays more and more people throng the highways leading into Africa's major cities (above). But most Africans still live in countless small, dusty villages, such as those in Zaïre (top right) and Mali (lower right).

THE PEOPLE

As they have for generations, African villagers draw strength and satisfaction from their own group's traditions. Their rituals may include the joyous celebration which takes place before a hunt (left) or the solemn funeral march which marks a village death (below).

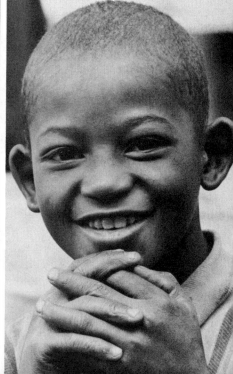

FACES: Far from resembling one another, Africans
have a wide variety of physical features. Clockwise
from top left: Indian fishermen of East Africa, white
diamond miners of South Africa, San young people, a
Malgache boy, and a Tutsi dancer of central Africa.

CHANGES: *Devotion to tradition is not enough to keep African customs exactly as they are. Some signs of change: a labor union meeting in Lesotho (left), a vaccination for a Nigerian chief (above), and a shopping tour in a shiny new Botswana supermarket.*

THE ECONOMY

Threatened by sluggish soil and fickle rains, many African villagers must struggle to keep their food supply in balance. Some herd cattle, following the rains to places where the grass is thickest. But most are farmers, working to the timeless tune of pick and plow.

SKILLS: In growing numbers, Africans are
finding that special skills pay off in
better jobs. Some who already have such
skills: workers at a Kinshasa factory
(above), a teacher in Senegal (upper right),
and field hands on a Kenya farm (right).

MAKING WAVES: Of all the continents, Africa has the greatest resources for turning water into electricity. Despite sites such as Kariba Dam (above), this potential is mostly untapped. Yet electricity is needed to run industries such as lumbering (right) and copper mining (below). These needs make dam-building a wave of the future.

THE CULTURE

Since Africa has few written languages, little of its history has been set down in writing. Thus, Africans must look elsewhere for clues to their past. Many clues lie hidden in ancient relics. Two of them: the stone ruins of old Zimbabwe* (left) and a plaque (below) showing a king of ancient Benin in western Africa.

TIMING: African music often makes use of complex rhythms, celebrated here by a village dancer in Senegal (far left), a ceremonial drummer in Ghana (left), and a parade in Kenya (below).

PATTERNS: Each African ethnic group has its own flair for design. Styles vary from the sharp features of a Cokwe mask (above) to the rounded look of Masai jewelry (upper right) to the playful patterns which adorn a Cameroon *house (far right). Art objects such as the finely crafted sculpture of antelopes (right) are often used in religious rites.

4
WINDS
OF
CHANGE

Chapter 10

Africa in the Modern World

SOMEWHERE IN AFRICA a lone young man walks silently down a dirt road in the heat of early afternoon. In one hand he lugs a canvas suitcase, and in the other he swings a walking stick. Behind him lies the peaceful village of his childhood. Ahead, on the horizon, rise the dim outlines of a city he has never seen until this moment.

He is leaving his village and moving to the city in search of a better life. He may be traveling only a few short miles. Yet, in what he is about to experience, he might as well be moving continents away.

Within a few days he will be making a new home and meeting new friends. Within a few weeks he will be eating new foods and buying new clothes. Nothing in his life will ever seem quite the same. He will never be able to retrace entirely the steps he is about to take.

His journey is similar to others made by millions of African villagers, both men and women, in recent years. In a sense this journey is symbolic. It symbolizes the break with many features of the past now being made all across the continent. For Africa is not a timeless and unchanging land. Now more than ever it is a continent buffeted by the winds of change.

These winds have blown hardest down the broad boulevards of Africa's modern cities. But they have reached into isolated villages as well. They are coming from all directions — from Europe, from Asia, from the Americas, and from other parts of Africa itself. Wherever they come from, they have brought great changes to the ways Africans lead their lives.

What are some of these changes? Let's take a closer look at three of them and see what they have meant to the people of the continent:

Religion. Throughout history most Africans have been animists (see page 50). Six out of 10 still are today. But other religions have also made inroads on the continent. One of the most widespread is Islam.

This faith springs from the teachings of an Arab named Mohammed,* who lived in the seventh century. Mohammed stressed belief in one Supreme Being, known as Allah.* Moslems consider Mohammed to have been Allah's Messenger on earth. They believe that Allah's words, as heard by Mohammed, were written down in a holy book, the Koran.*

Mohammed's teachings were spread across North Africa as early as the eighth century. Islam has been pushing slowly southward ever since. Today the influence of Islam is felt deep in central Africa. Two out of 10 people in Tropical and Southern Africa consider themselves Moslems.

Why has Islam had such a wide appeal? As it hap-

☙ Two out of 10 people in Tropical and Southern Africa consider themselves Moslems.

Moslem faithful say their prayers in a mosque (house of worship) in Addis Ababa, Ethiopia.

pens, many of Mohammed's teachings mix easily with traditional African beliefs. According to the Koran, for example, a man may take as many as four wives at once. This practice matches the customs of many African groups, which have permitted polygyny for centuries.

Whatever the reasons, Islam has found a firm following on the African continent. So too has Christianity. Ethiopia has been a Christian country since the fourth century. But elsewhere in Tropical and Southern Africa, Christianity arrived much later.

It was carried there by European missionaries, who began going to Africa in large numbers at the end of the 18th century. In 1792 a group of English Baptists formed the London Missionary Society to spread the gospel on African soil. Soon similar societies were being formed by other groups — Protestant and Roman Catholic alike. Their work has continued steadily for nearly two centuries.

But this work has been complicated by the fact that not all Christian teachings mix easily with older African beliefs. African animists, for instance, place great stress on ancestor worship, but Christian doctrines regard these beliefs as superstitions. Nonetheless, Christianity has gained steadily in popularity among Africans — especially among African leaders. This has largely been because of the influence of Christian mission schools. Nowadays about two out of every 10 people in Tropical and Southern Africa regard themselves as Christians.

Education. Until the 19th century, African education was pretty much a family affair. Young people were taught by their relatives the duties they would perform as adults. In addition, cult schools prepared young people for their roles in traditional societies. Only a tiny handful of Africa's many languages existed in written form. So there was little or no need to train young people to read or write.

Such teaching began with the coming of European missionaries. It started for the simplest of reasons. Before missionaries could explain their religions, they had to be able to communicate with the Africans they wanted to convert. Thus, English missionaries taught their African students English, French missionaries taught French, and so on.

By the early 20th century, mission schools had spread all across Africa. Also, after the Europeans set up African colonies (see page 168), colonial governments aided these schools or created schools of their own. At least one group, the Kikuyu of East Africa, also started a local school system. Such efforts planted the urge for education firmly among the African people.

What has happened to that urge since African nations began to win independence in the 1950's? For the most part it has continued. To be sure, most African nations still lack enough teachers to provide an education for all who wish it. They also lack the money to build enough new schools.

But, in spite of these difficulties, education has kept on growing. In many countries the number of young people attending school has doubled and even tripled since independence. To Africans this is one of their greatest achievements.

Urbanization. No change has been more far-reaching than urbanization (the growth of cities). In fact, Africa's cities have been the seedbed for many other changes which have swept the continent as a whole. The growth of cities has fed the urge for education. And it has helped to alter old beliefs, values, and customs in many ways.

Compared with some ancient cities of Europe and

✌§ In many African countries the number of young people attending school has doubled and even tripled.

Asia, most African cities are young upstarts. Nairobi,* the capital of Kenya, is a case in point. It was nothing more than a water hole for Masai herdsmen until about 1896. In that year the British government began building a rail line linking the city of Mombasa on the East African coast with Uganda in the interior. Soon Nairobi was a small trading center along the rail route. Today it has become a hub of commerce for all East Africa.

Similar examples could be found among the cities of West Africa. A few of them date back before the days of the European penetration. But many West African cities are of recent vintage. Like Nairobi, many were built by Europeans, who used them as centers of trade.

Most African cities are still commercial centers. Many of their busy side streets are lined with warehouses and their harbors with wharves. Generally these cities also have a number of light industries. Their factories may produce bricks or bicycle bells or clothing of many different kinds.

Heavy industry is much harder to find. A few cities have it — the copper-smelting city of Lubumbashi,* in Zaïre, for example, and bustling Lagos in Nigeria. But the continent is a long way from being industrialized. One reason is that most African governments lack the wealth necessary to get industries under way.

Nonetheless, light industries have begun to flourish

Compare this classroom in Kenya with your own. How do the two seem similar? How do they differ?

⊷§ Cut off from their villages, many Africans remain strangers in the city. Unwilling to go backward, unable to go forward, they learn simply to survive.

in many cities. Indeed, for many years the industries have been drawing villagers to the cities like magnets. For industries offer jobs and relatively high salaries which villagers cannot obtain at home. So young people continue to pack their bags, say good-bye to their families, and head where they believe the opportunities are.

Once they arrive, they usually find city life a lot less glamorous than they had expected. Not for them are the expensive apartments which decorate the main boulevards. Instead, most find shelter amid the shacks and shanties of the slums. Many live in houses made of crates and cardboard and bits of tin. Some of these people quickly turn against the city and decide to go home.

Those who remain may face other difficulties. Some will find they do not have the skills necessary to get the jobs they want. To work in city shops, for example, most need to speak a European language. Villagers who do not know such languages often have to settle for unskilled jobs, and even these can be hard to find.

Then too there are the many complications of city life. People who have always traded by barter must learn to handle money. People who have always obeyed village laws must contend with city laws they do not completely understand. People who have always respected their families must often turn family members away from city quarters because of lack of space. Old values collide with new conditions in the cities. Some of these values are slowly fading away.

As they do, many urban Africans become people set adrift. They have lost many old values without finding new ones to replace them. Cut off from their villages, they remain strangers in the city. Unwilling to go backward, unable to go forward, they learn simply to survive.

Their loneliness is sometimes eased by membership in ethnic associations. These are social clubs whose members belong to the same ethnic group. Such clubs allow their members a chance to relax among people who speak the same language. They also help to maintain ties between the city and the villages left behind. In this way they help to bridge the gap between past and present.

More bridges may be needed. But newcomers to the city can be thankful that some already do exist. Such associations remind urban Africans of their yesterdays. And this can prepare them for their encounter with tomorrow.

People all over Africa rejoiced in the 1960's as one
territory after another gained independence from colonial
rule. This scene shows Independence Day, 1966, in Botswana.

COLONIALISM
AND
INDEPENDENCE

Take up the White Man's burden —
Send forth the best ye breed —
Go bind your sons to exile
 To serve your captives' need;
To wait, in heavy harness,
 On fluttered folk and wild —
Your new-caught, sullen peoples,
 Half-devil and half-child.

WHEN BRITISH WRITER Rudyard Kipling penned those
lines in 1899, he was trying to defend colonial rule. His
aim was to inspire Americans to spread their civilization

to their newly won Asian territory, the Philippines. Yet his poem, "The White Man's Burden," also served to inspire Europeans who were colonizing another part of the globe — Africa.

Back in those days most Europeans believed that they had the only worthwhile civilization. Like Kipling, they thought they had a mission to transplant their way of life to foreign lands. Few Europeans cared much what the people of Africa might think about being made to live by the white man's ways. They thought that Europeans had a responsibility. Believing that their ways were superior, they felt it was their responsibility to "civilize" the world.

Today this attitude seems old-fashioned, even a little blind. The "message" in Kipling's poem is now out of style. But the poem itself lives on as an example of the thinking of another age. It helps to explain why Europeans got so caught up in a scramble for Africa in the first place — and why they were finally forced to quit.

The scramble had begun as early as 1652, two centuries before Kipling's time. In that year a small band of Dutch settlers found their way to the southern tip of Africa and began to put down roots. In time descendants of these settlers helped to organize what is now the Republic of South Africa. But their story differs markedly from that of other settlers in Africa, and so it must be separately told (see page 200).

Elsewhere on the continent, the first major step toward colonialism took place in the late 1700's. In 1792 the British set up the first of three tiny colonies along the Gulf of Guinea in West Africa. In the early 1800's, these colonies became important bases in the British move to halt the slave trade. Meanwhile, the French set up a similar colony farther down the coast.

Once Europeans had a toehold in Africa, they realized how little they knew about it. So they set out to educate themselves. Throughout the 19th century European explorers crisscrossed the length and breadth of Africa, mapping its terrain. One of the most famous among them was a Scottish missionary named Dr. David Livingstone.

Livingstone was the first to trace the route of the Zambezi River in southern Africa in 1855.

Eleven years later Livingstone set off on another lonely journey into the heart of the continent. For five years the outside world heard nothing of him, and many thought he was dead. The *New York Herald* sent an adventurous young reporter, Henry Morton Stanley, to hunt for the missing explorer. In 1871 friends guided Stanley to a settlement on the banks of Lake Tanganyika* in East Africa. There, in a moment of high drama, Stanley found a lean-looking man in gray trousers and a shirt with red sleeves.

"Doctor Livingstone, I presume?" asked Stanley.

Livingstone simply answered, "Yes."

For a short time the two men did their exploring together; then they went their separate ways. When Livingstone died two years later, Stanley took up the missionary's work of exploration. Stanley's travels took him all the way from Zanzibar* in the east to the mouth of the Zaïre River (then called the Congo River) in the west. With his newsman's gift for turning phrases, Stanley wrote many thousands of words describing his journeys. His stories caught the imagination of readers far and wide.

They especially fascinated the king of one small European country, Leopold II of Belgium. Leopold led a people who made up in pride what they lacked in size. For centuries the Belgians had sat on the sidelines while other European powers searched for new worlds to conquer. Now, inspired by Stanley's tales of wealth along the Congo, Leopold decided to do some searching of his own.

In 1879 Leopold sent Stanley back to the Congo as his agent. Stanley's assignment was to create a personal empire for Leopold in the area. For the next five years Stanley traveled about the region, bargaining with African chiefs. By the time he had finished, he had brought within Leopold's control a territory 75 times larger than Belgium itself.

Stanley's success set off an intense rivalry among sev-

COLONIAL AFRICA IN 1914

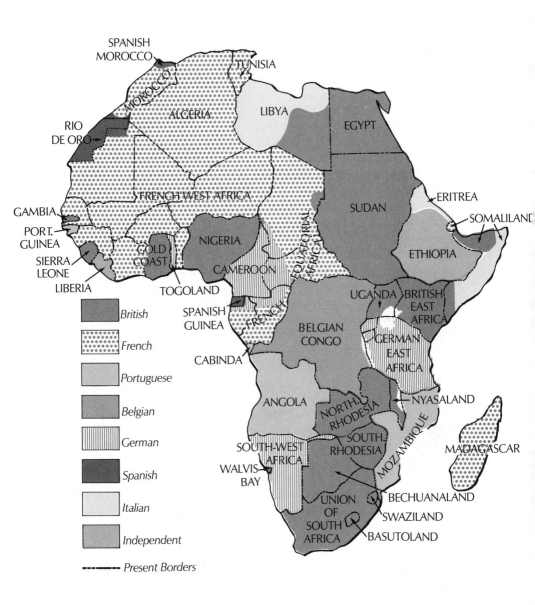

SPANISH
MOROCCO

TUNISIA

MOROCCO

ALGERIA

LIBYA

EGYPT

RIO
DE ORO

FRENCH WEST AFRICA

SUDAN

ERITREA

SOMALILAND

GAMBIA

PORT.
GUINEA

NIGERIA

GOLD
COAST

CAMEROON

EQUATORIAL AFRICA

ETHIOPIA

SIERRA
LEONE

LIBERIA

TOGOLAND

SPANISH
GUINEA

FRENCH

UGANDA

BRITISH
EAST
AFRICA

CABINDA

BELGIAN
CONGO

GERMAN
EAST
AFRICA

ANGOLA

NORTH.
RHODESIA

NYASALAND

SOUTH.
RHODESIA

MOZAMBIQUE

MADAGASCAR

SOUTH-WEST
AFRICA

WALVIS-
BAY

BECHUANALAND

SWAZILAND

UNION
OF
SOUTH
AFRICA

BASUTOLAND

British

French

Portuguese

Belgian

German

Spanish

Italian

Independent

------- Present Borders

eral European powers. One by one they gobbled up bite-sized chunks of the African map. Germany gained control of a section of East Africa and three areas in West Africa (Togoland* in the north, the Cameroons in the center, and South-West Africa to the south). France grabbed up most of the grassy areas of West Africa between the Sahara and the rain forests of the tropics. Portugal widened its boundaries in Angola.* Britain established colonies in East Africa, and enlarged its colonies farther north along the West African coast.

The results were astounding. When the race for Africa began in the late 1870's, nearly the entire continent had been independent. Less than 25 years later, only two major areas remained so. One was the West African republic of Liberia,* founded in 1822 by freed black slaves from the U.S. The other was the ancient empire of Ethiopia in East Africa.

In many cases the European "conquerors" were merely military officers who had hired black troops to make a show of force. Their hastily assembled "armies" marched into village after village to assert control. The officers would tell bewildered villagers that they now owed their loyalty to a white ruler in some far-off land. In this way, new border lines were drawn helter-skelter across the face of Africa, often dividing once-united peoples.

Once these "armies" had marched through, European settlers sometimes followed. But the settlers tended to be choosy about where they lived. In general, they shunned West Africa where the heat was oppressive and pests such as mosquitoes and tsetse flies carried deadly diseases. Far more popular were the higher, cooler plains of East Africa, located outside the "mosquito barrier."

While Europeans were moving onto the continent, their home governments were exerting greater and greater control over African life. These governments took an especially strong hand in the economy of the area. In Britain and Belgium special companies were given exclusive power over trade and mining in certain regions. Most of these companies remained closely linked to whatever European government had established them. And they acted in the interests of Europeans, not Africans.

Trade between Africa and Europe expanded greatly. The trouble was that this trade did little to help Africans develop their own industries. Africans brought to this trade their raw materials — metals, for example, or cocoa beans. In exchange they imported clothing and other finished products from the factories of Europe.

To be sure, Africans did reap some benefits from the coming of the Europeans. New schools were started, new roads were laid, new dams were built. Yet for Africans the drawbacks of colonialism clearly outweighed the advantages. Most of all, Africans resented being "made over" by outsiders.

The result was a smoldering sense of ill will. For many Africans the obvious question was, Why couldn't they govern themselves? Some began forming political movements aimed at freeing black colonies from European rule. Yet these movements simmered for half a century without yielding important results.

Then came World War II in Europe (1939-45). During the war many Africans fought for the European powers — some in Europe and some in North Africa. Fighting alongside Europeans, black Africans soon discovered that white men were not the superior people they were supposed to be. Many of these Africans returned home much more determined to end the white man's rule.

Under other circumstances their determination might have led nowhere. But the war had weakened the nations of Europe to the point of near-collapse. Now the old colonial powers could no longer afford costly efforts to hold their colonies together. Moreover, millions of Europeans had fought in World War II to preserve their freedom from Nazi Germany. After the war, they were naturally more sympathetic to cries for independence from their colonies overseas.

And so, around the world, the white man began to lay his "burden" down. In 1946 the U.S. granted independence to the Philippines. The next year Britain set India free. In Africa hopes for independence rose higher and higher. In the following decade those hopes finally bore fruit.

The first African colony to go independent was a British possession, the Gold Coast in West Africa. In 1957 the Gold Coast became the self-governing nation of Ghana. Then, over the next 15 years, Europeans gave up colonial leadership in one part of Africa after another.

Again and again the same ritual would unfold. Bands would play. Fireworks would light up the African sky. Finally, at midnight, the colonial flag would be lowered, and a new flag would rise in its place. All of this would usually be done to chants such as *"Uhuru"** (the Swahili word for "freedom").

Now old hopes for independence gave way to new hopes for a better way of life. These new hopes were not so easily achieved. In the decade after independence, civil wars wracked two of Africa's largest nations, Zaïre and Nigeria. Coups or other disturbances took place in more than half of Africa's black-ruled nations. But whatever the problems, Africans could at last feel that they were shaping their own destiny. The era of colonialism was over — to the vast relief of Africans. And Europeans were coming to understand that in many ways the "white man's burden" had really been a "black man's burden" all along.

Double-check

Review

1. Along with animism, what two main religions have found a firm following in Africa?

2. What has happened to the number of African young people attending school in many countries since independence?

3. What growth has been the seedbed for many other changes which have swept the African continent?

4. Once Europeans had a toehold in Africa in the 1800's what did they realize?

5. When and by whom was Liberia founded?

Discussion

1. Why might it be difficult for an African villager to adjust to life in a large city? What ideas can you suggest that might make the adjustment easier?

2. Is switching from rural to city life easier — or harder — for people in the U.S. than for people in Africa? Give reasons for your answer.

3. In what ways was the "white man's burden" really the "black man's burden"?

Activities

1. Some students might research Islam, Christianity, and a few traditional African religions and then report to the rest of the class on basic beliefs and practices — and similarities and differences — of each.

2. One group of students might role-play a team of 19th-century European missionaries to an African village. Other students could play the parts of villagers who have just learned of the missionaries' arrival. What would the first 15 minutes of conversation be?

3. Some students might draw political cartoons illustrating some aspect of colonialism and/or independence on the African continent. Others might pretend to be African students, writing letters to European friends explaining their desire for independence and their hopes for the future of their nation. Still others might try writing poetic parodies of, or answers to, Kipling's poem, "The White Man's Burden."

Skills

Rothco

Vadillo–El Sol De Mexico

Use the political cartoon above and information in Chapter 10 to answer the following questions.

1. Whom does the man in the chair represent? Whom does the man beating the drum represent?

2. What is causing the man in the chair to shake?

3. What "message" do you think the man is sending on the drum?

4. What seems to be the main point of this cartoon?

5. What do you think is the cartoonist's opinion about the African independence movement discussed in Chapter 10?

Chapter 11

An Avenue Named Uhuru

LONG AGO, according to legend, God summoned a man named Kikuyu to the top of Mount Kenya. He told Kikuyu to look down at the rivers, forests, and herds of wild animals on the land below. He showed him the fertile hills which rolled out from the base of the mountain. Then, the legend says, God gave these rich highlands to Kikuyu to settle and cultivate.

Today the descendants of Kikuyu number in the millions. Of Kenya's more than 70 ethnic groups, the Kikuyu is the largest. Most of the Kikuyu people still live in "Kikuyuland" — the fertile highlands given them in the legend. They depend on this land for their livelihood, raising crops and livestock, and they cherish it as the home of their ancestors.

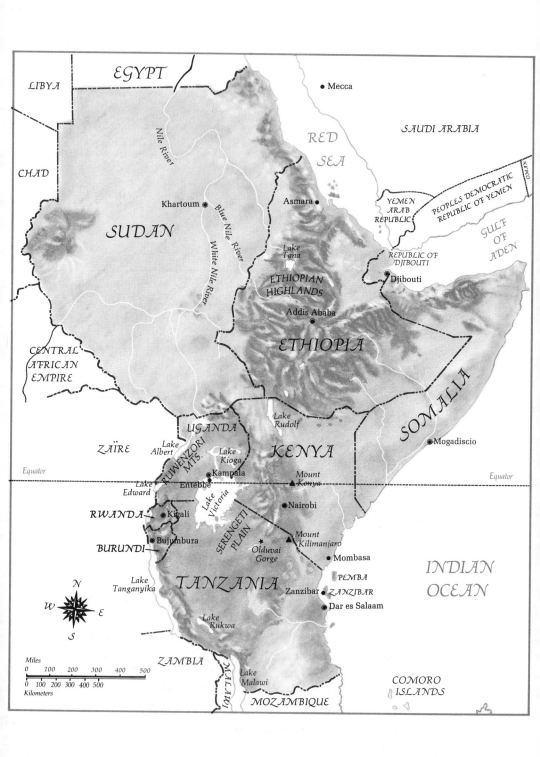

Eighteen-year-old Mugendi* lived with his family in a small village in the west of Kikuyuland. The snowy summit of Mount Kenya loomed on the horizon, some 50 miles to the north. A few hours away by footpath and road was the town of Muranga* and the railroad which brought trains creeping up from Nairobi, Kenya's capital city.

Mugendi received most of his education in the traditional way — from his parents and his daily experiences. He learned the history of his village and clan. He learned how time and tradition and common sense had woven networks of personal relationships which held his ethnic group together. He learned dignity and respect for others as well as for himself.

Out in the green pastureland, Mugendi herded goats and sheep. He could tell at a glance if even one goat in a herd of 50 or 100 was missing. His father, Karenga,* gave him a piece of land for growing corn and beans. And Karenga taught his son all he knew of the complex rituals and laws of conduct of the Kikuyu people.

When Mugendi was 17, he had undergone initiation ceremonies to become a full member of his community. He was now officially a man, with the right to own property, build his own house, and, if he chose, look for a suitable wife.

Several months after the initiation ceremony, Karenga gave his son a few sheep and goats to start a herd of his own. As the herd grew, so would Mugendi's wealth and status among the people of his village. In addition to herding these animals, Mugendi was expected to help with the planting and cultivation of his family's gardens. His family raised corn and beans, potatoes, millet, peas, and several other vegetables. Though Mugendi helped with planting, only the women of the family picked these crops.

✑ Out in the green pastureland, Mugendi herded goats and sheep. He could tell at a glance if even one goat in a herd of 50 or 100 was missing.

The members of Mugendi's family ate only what they grew themselves. They rarely had any extra food to sell or trade in the market for cloth, tools, or other goods. Karenga had no desire to acquire unnecessary goods for his family or himself. He was content to work his lands, watch his herds increase, and take part in the activities of his family, clan, and community.

Mugendi, however, was restless. At village ceremonies and feasts he had come to know a girl named Wanjiku.* In recent weeks they had flirted, laughed, and danced together more and more often. Mugendi had grown very fond of Wanjiku, and he would have liked to take the first ritual steps toward marrying her. But he could not because he had not yet acquired the necessary wealth.

Like the members of most African ethnic groups, a Kikuyu tribesman and his family must give valuable goods to the family of his intended bride. Traditionally, the Kikuyu bride-price is at least 30 goats or sheep, or three cows. But Mugendi had only nine goats and three sheep, no more than his father had given him a year before. Several kids and lambs were born during the year but two of these had been taken by a leopard. He had also had to pay a fine of one goat to his neighbors for going walking with Wanjiku rather than helping them put up a new hut.

Mugendi's herd was large for a man his age. At 18 he would normally not need the bride-price for marriage for another seven or eight years. But in recent years, Kikuyu men had begun to marry earlier. They earned the bride-price by leaving their villages and finding jobs in the cities or on the huge plantations of the Europeans.

Mugendi knew several young men who had done this. He envied them when they had come strutting back to the village wearing European-style trousers with coins jingling in the pockets. Some rode new bicycles or carried transistor radios which blared out popular songs. Mugendi also saw how these men were admired by the girls of the village.

One of Mugendi's closest friends was Moigai.* Moigai had just returned from Nairobi where in six months he had earned enough money to buy a herd of 50 goats. Often in the evenings the two friends would sit together around the cooking fire in Moigai's hut and talk about what Moigai had seen and done away from the village.

Moigai told Mugendi that when he had first seen Nairobi he had thought that Ngai,* God Himself, must have built it. He described the city's tall buildings, its double-decker buses, and the electric lights that sparkled everywhere at night. He talked about the city's strange-looking women who wore their hair long instead of shaving their heads in the traditional Kikuyu fashion.

Moigai had originally left for Nairobi with hardly a penny in his pocket. He walked the 50 miles of bumpy roads to the capital in two days. Once in the city, he stayed with cousins in a large modern housing project built by the government. The two-story apartments were very different from the round Kikuyu huts he was used to. But, like the huts, each had an indoor fireplace for cooking and warming during the cool highland nights. At the back door, each fam-

ily had a small plot to grow vegetables. Moigai soon felt quite at home.

Moigai learned that most jobs of any kind were hard to find, even for Africans who could speak English. He could speak only Kikuyu and Swahili, the language widely used throughout East Africa. Luckily, however, a few days before he arrived an Indian shopkeeper had asked his cousin if he knew of someone who could help out in his store. The Indian preferred newcomers to the city, for he felt they were apt to be more honest and industrious. Moigai laughed when he heard this — and decided to see the shopkeeper.

From the street, the shop appeared to be small, but on the inside the display room stretched back like a hallway into a gloomy interior. Walls and racks on every side were hung with rugs of all kinds. There were animal skins as well as handmade or manufactured rugs of wool, rope, cotton, and synthetic fibers. Besides the rugs, the owner had a glass case full of costume jewelry that twinkled on display near the front of the shop.

Moigai agreed to sweep, dust, run errands, and do odd jobs for the equivalent of $20 a month. The shop was open six days a week from eight to seven. Like all the others, it closed for a two-hour lunch break starting at noon.

The totally new surroundings made the work interesting enough for Moigai. Occasionally, Kikuyu men and women came into the store, and the owner would ask Moigai to give a sales talk in the Kikuyu language. But most customers were either Europeans or Asians.

Throughout Africa, the life of the village and the life of the city are worlds apart. Above, a Kikuyu village. Below, a street in Nairobi.

◄§ At first, Karenga refused to permit his son to leave. Why was Mugendi unhappy with his life in the village? Why did he want to go to the white man's city?

Most of the Asians were Indians like the owner of the shop. Many of them had lived in Nairobi all their lives. The Europeans, on the other hand, were generally wealthy tourists. They came to the shop to buy zebra rugs or the skins of other wild animals.

Moigai had to learn to be careful with his money. It took him nearly two months to save enough to buy a small radio. The wealth of the city people amazed him. He sometimes sold white men and women three or four zebra skins at a time. They paid more for each of the skins than Moigai earned in three months.

Everything that Moigai had to say about Nairobi fascinated Mugendi. He liked best to hear the tales of city girls, dance bands, and noisy motorcycles. But he was also excited by the stories of other Kikuyu men who were becoming rich and famous in the city.

Moigai also spoke of his loneliness since he was so far from his family and village. It was this loneliness that had led Moigai to return to the village after only six months. He had come back intending to use his savings to buy sheep and goats. Then he would marry and settle into the life of his father and his father before him.

But now, the more he talked about city life with Mugendi, the more restless Moigai became to go back to it. Perhaps if Mugendi came to Nairobi with him, they could share a room and get jobs together. Together there would be no loneliness, and they would have a fine time.

The two young men discussed this plan deep into

People of many different backgrounds mingle in downtown Nairobi. What other aspects of life in East Africa's cities does this photo reveal?

the night for weeks. In June, Mugendi finally made up his mind that he must go with Moigai to Nairobi. The big rains were almost over and soon the women would begin the harvest. His father was content. It was a good time for Mugendi to tell him of his plans.

At first, Karenga refused to permit his son to leave. He was more puzzled by the plan than angry. Why was Mugendi unhappy with his life in the village? Why did he want to go to the white man's city? Had not Moigai grown unhappy there after only six months? Had not Mugendi seen how city life had turned some of his other friends into fools? How they now listened only to their radios, and never to their fathers? How they laughed at the most sacred customs of the Kikuyu people?

Mugendi did not tell his father about his envy for these "fools." But he did remind him that Moigai was now eager to return to Nairobi and that they would go together. He argued that Nairobi was no longer a "white man's city." He said that Moigai had seen blacks who lived in fine houses there. He mentioned that the broad avenues now had African names such as Uhuru (freedom).

Mugendi added that no temptation from the white man's world could turn him from his people. He did not plan to settle in the city. He only planned to spend a few months there. He would return with money to buy a herd of goats and sheep, and perhaps to take a bride. Soon, he predicted, there would be a grandson for Karenga.

"I will not forbid you to go," Karenga said. "I see you will go anyway and it will be easier for you with my blessing. Only do not forget your obligations to us. We will welcome you when you return."

Mugendi sold most of his herd to have some money for a start in the city. He also took with him several necklaces and belts of ornamental beadwork made by his sisters. Moigai said that he could sell these to Europeans in Nairobi for a good price if he needed more money later. He wrapped them in a goatskin, along with an old pair of shorts, placed the bundle on his head, and followed Moigai down the footpath toward Muranga. He kept looking back until finally they crossed over a ridge and he could no longer see his village or the snowy crest of Mount Kenya.

Double-check

Review

1. How many ethnic groups live in Kenya? Which group is the largest?

2. What did Mugendi learn from his traditional education?

3. At what age did Mugendi become a full member of his community? What rights did this give him?

4. Why did Mugendi not take the first ritual steps toward marrying Wanjiku?

5. Why did Mugendi have to pay a fine of one goat to his neighbors?

Discussion

1. Karenga thought that city life had turned some of Mugendi's friends into fools. Do you think Mugendi was foolish to want to live in Nairobi? Why, or why not? Do you think he will return home soon? If not, why not?

2. In what ways does this chapter illustrate the importance of family and community to African people? Are such relationships important in your community? Explain your answer.

3. Why might the shopkeeper have felt that newcomers to Nairobi would be more honest and hardworking than others? Do you agree with this view? Are African and U.S. cultures both suspicious of "city" people? Should they be? Why, or why not?

Activities

1. Will Mugendi be led astray in the big city? Will Wanjiku forget all about him? What will happen? Several students might write their own versions of Mugendi's life in the big city and Wanjiku's life in the village. Afterward they could read their stories aloud, and the rest of the class could vote on which version they think is what probably will happen.

2. Kenya's first president was Jomo Kenyatta, a charismatic and controversial leader during turbulent times in Africa. Some students might research and report on his life and leadership in Kenya.

3. Students who hold differing views on the subject might stage an informal debate in front of the class on small-village versus big-city life. Each debator could begin his or her presentation by saying: "It is better to grow up and live in a small village [big city] because. . . ."

Skills

URBANIZATION IN EAST AFRICA

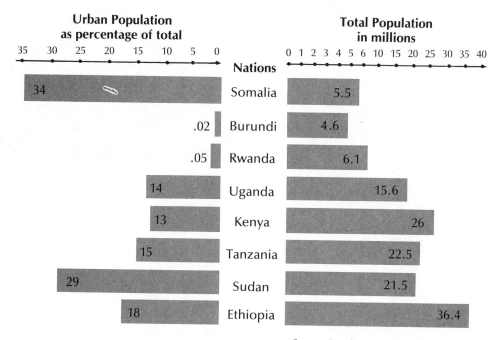

Urban Population as percentage of total

Total Population in millions

Nations	Urban %	Total (millions)
Somalia	34	5.5
Burundi	.02	4.6
Rwanda	.05	6.1
Uganda	14	15.6
Kenya	13	26
Tanzania	15	22.5
Sudan	29	21.5
Ethiopia	18	36.4

Source: Population Reference Bureau

Use the bar graph above and information in Chapter 11 to answer the following questions.

1. What do the bars on the right represent? The bars on the left?

2. Which of the above countries has the largest population? Which two countries have almost the same population?

3. Which country has the lowest percentage of its population living in urban areas?

4. In which country do about 300,000 people live in urban areas?

5. If Mugendi traveled in a straight line, roughly how many miles would he have to travel to get from his new home to the capital of East Africa's most urbanized country?

5
CULTURES IN CONFLICT

NON-WHITES NIE-BLANKES

Chapter 12

In White-ruled Africa

MOST OF AFRICA south of the Sahara is now ruled by black Africans. Many young children growing up in Africa do not remember the time when white foreigners ruled most of this area. However, there is one country — at the southern tip of Africa — where black children never forget that whites are still in control. This country is the Republic of South Africa.

Until the 1950's, Europeans still ruled most of what is today independent black Africa (see pages 168-174). Then one African colony after another gained its independence from the old colonial powers. A recent new nation — Zimbabwe — gained its independence from Great Britain in 1980.

South Africa is an independent nation too. But unlike most of its neighbors, South Africa is dominated by its white population. Whites make up only about

◄§ Black Africans are allowed to work in white areas by day, but are required to return at night to black-only areas or towns near the white cities.

15 percent of the 32.5 million people living in South Africa—but the whites run the civil service, the police force, the army, and most of the large businesses in the country.

Why are whites still in control in South Africa? Why haven't the same "winds of change" that have brought black governments to the lands to the north toppled this white regime in southern Africa?

Part of the answer is that Africa has been home for many whites of South Africa for generations. Many white South Africans are descendants of people who settled on the southern tip of Africa more than a century before the American Revolution.

Most of the whites have no homeland to return to. They consider themselves permanent residents of South Africa, unlike many Europeans elsewhere in Africa who consider themselves merely temporary residents in a foreign land.

At home or not, these whites are vastly outnumbered by a black African majority. The whites know that majority rule, such as that practiced by the democratic nations of the world, would automatically mean black African rule. In order to prevent this, the government of South Africa has put restrictions on free political action.

In the cities of South Africa, almost every white family employs at least one black servant to care for the children and do housework.

Black Africans in South Africa are not allowed to vote in national elections or to run for national offices. Those who protest against government policies are liable to be arrested and jailed. Freedoms of speech, press, and assembly, which are enjoyed in many democratic countries of the world, are lacking in South Africa.

Whites exercise control over blacks in South Africa through a strict policy of segregation. South Africans call their race laws *apartheid*.* On the national level, apartheid means setting aside sections of the country for "independent" homelands, according to ethnic or tribal backgrounds. On the local level, apartheid means blacks living totally apart from whites.

In theory, whites are in charge of "white" areas, while the word of black people is supposed to be law in "black" areas. But the South African government continues to exercise strong influence over the homelands.

Some of the homelands, such as Transkei, have been granted independence by the South African government. Other countries around the world have refused to recognize Transkei and the other homelands. This is because these foreign governments do not approve of the apartheid policy. Also, the homelands lack enough resources to support large numbers of people. The areas have little mineral wealth and the land is often eroded and overgrazed by cattle. Furthermore, the South African government has reserved only 13 percent of the country's land for these homelands where over 70 percent of the population is supposed to live.

Since there are not enough jobs in the homelands, black Africans often go to the cities in white areas to work. They fill the need for cheap labor in white industries. Generally they have to take the most menial

In white-ruled South Africa, the government has
set aside certain areas for those black people
and their families who work in nearby white
cities. One of these black areas is shown above.

jobs. Blacks do not get the best-paying jobs nor the jobs that involve supervising white workers.

To the South African government, blacks are theoretically only "visitors" in white areas; they have the right to be in those areas only if employed there. The majority of South Africa's black population is employed in white areas. Black Africans are allowed to work in these areas by day, but most return at night to black-only areas or towns near the white cities. Some blacks commute nearly 200 miles daily to and from work.

Until 1986, blacks were required to carry passes with them whenever they were in a white area. Police could check their passes at any time.

Blacks cannot ride in white train cars or buses, or attend white schools. Because black schools are educationally inferior to white schools, many black students cannot get a competitive education. Many restaurants and beaches are only for white people. In white areas, black people cannot vote or hold certain jobs reserved for whites.

Supporters of apartheid point out that South Africa has spent a great deal of money demolishing slum shantytowns and building better housing for blacks. The literacy rate of blacks is higher in South Africa than elsewhere on the continent. Hospitals, schools, and clinics have been built. The average living standard of blacks in South Africa is unquestionably higher than that of blacks elsewhere in Africa.

Still, critics point out that the black African standard of living is well below that of whites. On the average, white workers earn ten times as much as black workers. (For a personal view of the situation in South Africa, see Chapter 13.)

In the past few years, there have been some cracks in the walls of apartheid. Until recently, sports—like almost everything else in South Africa—were strictly segregated. Now, because of international pressure, some black athletes from South Africa are being accepted on all-white teams. Even more importantly, the laws prohibiting marriage and relationships between blacks and whites have been repealed. Recently, South African President P.W. Botha promised to give South African citizenship to the residents of the impoverished tribal homelands.

These reforms have made a few cracks in the wall, but economics could well shake the wall to its foundation. As the South African economy expands, there is an ever-increasing need for skilled workers.

Under the laws of apartheid, only whites can hold the most skilled jobs. But there aren't enough skilled workers to go around. Thus, more and more blacks are being trained to fill the need. In recent years, blacks and people of mixed blood have been hired for skilled jobs in the gold mines and on the railroads. These jobs were traditionally reserved for white people only.

So far there have been only small changes in overall policy. Many white South Africans have made it clear that they will not abandon apartheid without a fight. But as blacks have gained an increasing role in the economic life of South Africa, they have increasingly demanded a share of political power.

Since 1976, there have been both peaceful and violent protests in South Africa against apartheid. In 1985, the country erupted in mass violence. Hundreds of blacks died that year in conflicts with the police and each other. The government declared a state of emergency in August. Blacks were no longer allowed to assemble even for peaceful purposes. Police harassed and beat them even during funeral processions.

The United States government has grown increasingly critical of South Africa's white supremacy. Many U.S. companies no longer wish to hold investments in South Africa. Some U.S. banks refuse to loan money to companies there. All this has made the South African government nervous. It no longer permits foreign journalists to photograph or videotape scenes of violence and protest, perhaps hoping to ease Western criticism of the regime.

Can the wealth and power of the white minority indefinitely hold down the black majority? Black Africans say no. They say that the white people of South Africa are perched on a time bomb and that the bomb is ticking away dangerously.

Some people wonder if South Africa will soon follow in the footsteps of Zimbabwe*. Formerly known as Rhodesia*, the country also had a white minority that controlled the nation's political and economic life.

Almost every white family in Rhodesia had its own house and a full-time servant or two. Many whites also had swimming pools or tennis courts. Most of the ranches in the beautiful countryside were owned by white families.

Civil war broke out in the 1970's between the Rhodesian government and several black nationalist groups. Almost 25,000 soldiers and civilians were killed during the seven-year conflict. The insurgent guerillas had the support of several neighboring countries—especially Zambia and Mozambique.

Finally, a cease-fire and democratic elections brought an end to the civil war. The election resulted in blacks dominating the new Zimbabwe government. Whites were given several ministerial posts as a sign that whites were welcome, and, in fact, encouraged to stay in the country. Though 60 percent of white Rhodesians fled upon independence, 100,000 remain. They have peacefully adapted to the new government.

Has the new Zimbabwe government been a success? Many people think so. Both black and white people in Zimbabwe have a good opinion of the new government. The country has been relatively prosperous recently. The harvests of 1985 were huge, allowing Zimbabwe to export food when most African nations had to import food. Unlike most African farmers, farmers in Zimbabwe can get free technical advice, fertilizer, and help in marketing their produce. They may also receive financial incentives from the government. All this contributes to successful farming.

So far, the main problem in Zimbabwe has been the violent clashes between two black ethnic groups—the Shona, who comprise about 77 percent of the black population, and the Ndbele*, who comprise 19 percent. The Ndbele believe that they do not have a fair share of political power, and it is said that they are responsible for certain guerilla attacks on people and property.

Looking at the Zimbabwe example, the world wonders what the future holds for South Africa. Will there be a blood bath—a civil war in which black nationalists fight white residents and soldiers of the South African government? Considering the desperate state of affairs there, many people believe a civil war is inevitable. However, the example of Zimbabwe has proven that African countries can recover from civil war and be well governed by a black majority.

*Tales of gold sped across South Africa in the late 1800's,
and men from many lands sought wealth beneath the earth.*

MIXED BLESSINGS
AND WINDS OF CHANGE

IN APRIL OF 1652, three small Dutch ships landed in a
bay near southern Africa's Cape of Good Hope. They
were packed with about 80 settlers and supplies. Under a
large, flat-topped mountain, the settlers laid out their settlement and began the task of growing food for themselves and for the Dutch trading vessels that stopped at
the harbor.

Life in the new settlement was hard and lonely. To
make a profit out of the land required a tough breed of
people. The settlers developed the belief that their
Bibles, their horses, and their guns were their best protection in the hostile land.

Over the years the original settlers died out and their
sons and daughters took over the land. As they did so,
they were joined by other Europeans from Holland,

France, and Germany. In time they stopped thinking of themselves as Dutch, or French, or German. Now they were *Afrikaners*,* ("Africans" in their language) or *Boers** (farmers). Slowly the number of Afrikaners expanded, and they began to push inland into the unknown continent.

At the beginning of the 19th century, a new force suddenly entered. Far away in Europe, Britain was at war with France, then ruled by Napoleon Bonaparte.* In order to protect the sea route to India, the British seized the Cape colony. They would remain in control for the next century.

The coming of the British upset the Afrikaner farmers. The British brought in strange ideas about the dignity of all men, regardless of color. They abolished slavery and set up courts where a servant could get equal justice with his master.

These steps may seem modest to us today, but to many of the Afrikaners they were outrageous. These Afrikaners resolved to get away from the British. Hundreds of families loaded their belongings on ox wagons and began a long and difficult trek (march) over the mountains into the unknown highlands. There they hoped to begin a new life free from British control. This movement is known as "the Great Trek." Like the move westward by the early American settlers, it has a deep meaning to white South Africans today.

But in escaping British rule, the Afrikaners came into direct conflict with another powerful people. For centuries, black African groups had been pushing southward from central Africa. At the time of the first white landing in 1652, the blacks had settled almost all of southern Africa. When the whites pushed northward, the result was war.

The blacks were great warriors, and they vastly outnumbered the whites. But the whites possessed rifles, horses, and even artillery. In the end the blacks were defeated and driven off much of their best land. By the 1870's, the white men were unchallenged rulers of most of southern Africa.

At this time, a chance discovery completely changed the course of South African history. In 1867 a diamond was discovered on the banks of the Orange River. Within days men began to rush to this barren area. Within months it had become a wide-open prospecting area.

A few years after the diamond rush, gold was discovered not far north. Another — and much larger — rush was on. From all over the world, men abandoned their jobs and families, and flocked to the gold fields. A sprawling mine camp sprang up around the mines. Today that mining camp is the city of Johannesburg* — with a population of more than two million, one of the largest cities in Tropical and Southern Africa.

This mining boom brought a steady stream of outsiders into the lands of the Afrikaners. Many of these outsiders were from Britain, and they served to increase conflicts between the Afrikaners and the British. The result was war between the whites. In the Anglo-Boer War of 1899-1902, the British emerged victorious and united all of southern Africa up to the Limpopo* River into one nation: the Union of South Africa.

With union, Afrikaner and English-speaking South Africans were forced into an uneasy partnership. Old suspicions remained, but they seemed less important as South Africa became strong and prosperous. An industrial revolution transformed it from a land of farmers into a major industrial nation.

For the black African, the development of an industrialized South Africa was a mixed blessing. On the one hand, the black worker in the mines or factories could earn far more than he could hope to make farming his parched land or tending his small herd. Thus millions of blacks left their homelands to flock to the cities.

On the other hand, the influx into the cities all but destroyed the traditional way of life based on closely knit families, clans, and communities, and on farming and herding. And the breakup of the old way of life hardened racial lines. Segregation became a way of life, enforced by both custom and law.

In the 1950's, the South African government began

passing apartheid laws designed to entrench white rule forever. The result was to keep whites and blacks apart in almost every aspect of social life. There were separate restaurants, theaters, churches, schools, even buses. To be sure, the whites continued to rely on black labor to work South African industry and to be personal servants.

☆ ☆ ☆ ☆ ☆ ☆ ☆ ☆ ☆

A hundred years ago, when the South African diamond fields first opened, a frail 18-year-old named Cecil Rhodes set off to make his fortune. Rhodes had gone out to Africa from England the year before to recover from tuberculosis. He threw himself into his work in the diamond diggings and almost immediately earned a small fortune. Not content with being rich, Rhodes then decided to get an education. He enrolled at Oxford University and spent the next few years traveling back and forth by boat between England (where he earned a degree) and South Africa (where he earned a few million dollars). He soon became a very powerful man.

Rhodes believed deeply that the British Empire was "the supreme achievement of history." He would have liked to have seen the whole world ruled by Britain. (At one time he even toyed with plans for Britain to annex the moon and the planets.) But for the moment, he had a more moderate scheme: extending British rule over all of Africa, from Cape Town to Cairo.

Events in Africa now seemed to bring that day closer. In 1890 a small group of whites organized by Rhodes settled the land to the north of the Limpopo River. Within three years, they controlled a wide area and had conquered a powerful native kingdom known as the Ndbele.* Soon white men were calling this land Rhodesia, after the founder.

Over the years, Rhodesia remained a colony of Britain, but the racial policy of its white minority was similar in many ways to its neighbor, South Africa. A small group of whites, outnumbered by blacks almost 20 to one, ruled the land and enforced a system of segregation. But the Rhodesian whites remained uneasy.

In the 1950's and '60's, they saw the "winds of change" sweeping over Africa to the north, and they feared the introduction of a black government in their country. In 1965 the whites took matters into their hands and declared themselves independent of Britain. Since Britain refused to accept this action, a prolonged dispute began. Britain argued that majority rule would have to come to Rhodesia eventually. Britain was supported in this view by the United Nations and by the United States.

Finally in 1980, Great Britain recognized Rhodesia's independence after free and open elections brought a black-dominated government to power. Now named Zimbabwe, the country is trying to serve the interests of the black community, while at the same time being fair to whites and encouraging them to stay.

Cecil Rhodes (right) and friends on an outing in 1897.

Double-check

Review

1. Whites make up about what percentage of the people living in South Africa?

2. What do South Africans call their race laws?

3. What finally brought an end to the civil war in Rhodesia?

4. Which European people first settled the Cape of Good Hope in 1652?

5. Who won the Anglo-Boer War of 1899-1902?

Discussion

1. What roles, if any, should people and/or nations outside of South Africa play in that nation's racial situation? For example, should world-famous black athletes go to South Africa for sports events? Should nations of the world refuse to trade with South Africa until it changes its racial laws? Should other nations recognize the "independence" of Transkei and other "homelands"? Give reasons to support your answers.

2. Do you think most white people will stay in Zimbabwe? Why, or why not? Should the government encourage them to stay?

3. Do you think the racial situation will change or remain the same in South Africa during your lifetime? If change comes, how will it come? If change does not come, how will it be prevented? Explain your answers.

Activities

1. Some students might draw political cartoons illustrating various aspects of life in South Africa or Zimbabwe, or some aspect of their relationships with other nations.

2. Two or more committees of students might be formed to research and report on the latest developments in Zimbabwe, South Africa, Namibia, Botswana, Madagascar, or one of the other countries in southern Africa. A file of newspaper clippings might be kept for each nation.

3. Some students might pretend to be famous athletes writing a letter to the South African government explaining why they will, or will not, come to South Africa to take part in a sports event. Volunteers might read their letters aloud to the rest of the class.

Skills

Use the political cartoon above and information in Chapter 12 to answer the following questions.

1. What does the tree in this cartoon symbolize?
  (a) South Africa   (b) an athletic event   (c) a high ideal

2. Whom do the people on the ground symbolize?
  (a) white Africans   (b) athletes   (c) black Africans

3. Whom does the man in the tree symbolize?
  (a) Tarzan
  (b) the government of South Africa
  (c) an American cowboy

4. With whom do you think the cartoonist is sympathetic?
  (a) the people on the ground   (b) the man in the tree   (c) neither

5. How would you express the message of this cartoon in your own words?

Chapter 13

A Pair of Shoes

PETER ZIMA* climbed wearily up the South African hillside, swung around, and dropped himself into the grass. He sat there with his arms around his knees and his head flopped forward, squinting out at the green blanket of pastureland below.

He could see three Xhosa* kraals* — clusters of small, round huts. Cattle dotted the expanse of open field between them. Smoke curled upward from a misty rise near the horizon. This scene had often brought contentment to Peter in the past. But today he could not forget the worries that had grown in him over the past few months.

Peter had always laughed at his friends when they left their Transkei* homeland in South Africa to work on white-owned farms or in the churning cities. Some went to the cities to find various unskilled jobs or to be servants in the homes of white families. But most ended up at the diamond holes of Kimberley or the gold shafts in Johannesburg. Peter had called them fools to leave their families for the dreary and dangerous work in the mines. But now he wished he had gone with them.

The reason was that Peter's friends now had money, and he did not. They returned from the city, often in a year or less, with cash enough to buy herds larger than Peter's. Some bought stoves and metal pots for their wives and wore expensive clothes. Peter did not greatly envy them for having these luxuries, but he did envy them for having cattle. For among the Xhosa people, cattle were the true symbol of a person's wealth and prestige.

By following the traditional life of the Xhosas, Peter was growing poorer, not richer. There had been too little rain this season, and the family vegetable garden had done badly. He had been forced to buy produce regularly at the expensive market. He'd sold two cows during the year to meet his expenses. Next week he would have to sell another to pay his taxes to the government of the Transkei homeland.

"Two calves born this year," Peter said to himself, "and three cows sold. So my life moves backward by one cow. I have no choice. I'll go to the mines."

There were no tears when Peter announced his decision to his family. He had talked of going before, and his wife understood the need. His father himself had once dug in the yellow dirt of Johannesburg. A younger brother had left to work in Cape Town a few months before. Indeed, so many men had left in search of jobs and money that Transkei was being called a homeland for women and children only.

The day after Peter sold his cow, he left the Xhosa kraal and made his way east toward Umtata,* the

**⊰ Down the shaft and into the dark
where ore was blasted and drilled.
Warm, heavy air. Helmet lights
on sweaty bodies and wet rock walls.**

South African miners drill for diamonds.

capital of the Transkei. As Peter neared Umtata, his thoughts turned more and more to the adventure that lay ahead. His friends had often told him about the backbreaking work in dark tunnels a mile underground. "Just one year," Peter promised himself. "Just one. If I can save all my pay, I'll have more than $500 and that will be enough."

Peter had been to Umtata before. It was a busy commercial center, far different from the sleepy kraals of his home. True, he was always awed by the town's large buildings and bustling traffic. But he remembered Umtata most for the nervous tightness that he felt as a black man on the streets of what was then a "white" city.

Peter's discomfort grew as he walked through the town. There was no flicker of friendship in the eyes of the blacks he passed. He became depressed and was on the verge of turning back, when he saw the labor recruiting office. He joined a small crowd of men milling about the door.

"Make your fortune in the city of gold," a grinning white man was telling them. "A free train ticket to Jo'burg for all volunteers. A loaf of bread and 30 cents to spend on the way."

Peter knew that the company offered these things to entice men to the mines. He also knew something that the recruiter didn't mention: Once at the mines, he would have to stay for at least a year. If he left, he would be caught and sent to jail. He forced himself to enter the office and then to board the train.

It was Peter's first train ride, and he enjoyed it. Leaving Umtata, the narrow railway car was less than half full. At each stop, more men piled into the car. Most of them were going all the way to the gold mines. From their talk, Peter knew they had been there before, some many times. Old friends met again

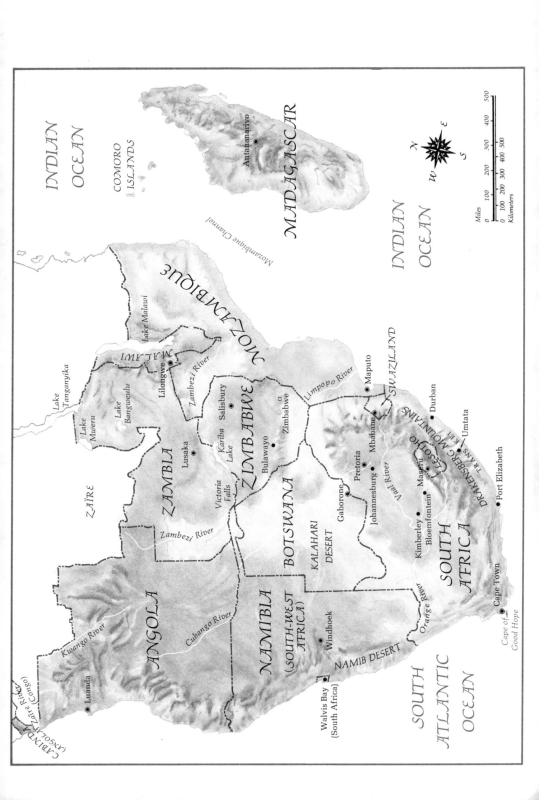

Winnie Mandela has been a leader in the fight against minority white rule in South Africa for 20 years. Her husband, Nelson, was jailed in 1964 for his political activism.

⊷§ On Saturdays, Peter stayed in the barracks. There he could sleep, talk, and play the guitar, or find someone to write a letter for him to his wife.

and laughed and teased each other. Some stood on the benches and danced to the rhythmic clack of the car's wheels.

It was dark when the train finally rolled to a stop in Johannesburg's Park Station. Peter followed the other men out of the car and onto the broad platform. Several black mine policemen grouped the men into columns and marched them out of the station.

Peter found himself in the heart of a city far greater than he had ever seen before. Lights blazed from windows stacked high into the sky. Shiny cars whizzed down crowded streets that seemed to have no end. The air itself almost pulsed with excitement. Slightly dazed, Peter climbed into the company bus that would take the miners to their living quarters.

Peter's bunk was one of 16 concrete slabs in a simple barracks room. A few of the men who shared the room were newcomers like himself, but most had already spent several months in the mines. He tried talking in the Xhosa language to some of the men in other barracks. They only shrugged. He learned later that these gold miners come not only from areas throughout South Africa but also from other parts of the continent. They are lured to the mines by the promise of steady work at comparatively good pay.

At dawn they marched two abreast out of the gates of the barracks to the entrance of the mine complex. A mine policeman stopped Peter and the other new arrivals at the gate. "Give me your passbooks," he said. Peter reached in his pocket for the thick booklet of identification which all black South Africans are required by law to carry.

"Wait here," the man said.

An hour later, he returned with special passes which would allow each of them to enter the mine. Peter's said simply: "Pass Native Zima." Below was written the name of the white man who would be his boss.

After a few days' training, Peter joined a "gang" of workmen and made his first trip down into the mine He had never before ridden an elevator, but even if he had, the "cage" would have taken him by surprise. There he stood one minute, looking out at the familiar mine structure. Suddenly there was a sharp warning whistle. Then the earth seemed to collapse beneath him.

He gasped and held his stomach as the elevator cage plummeted down thousands of feet in the next minute. Lights from the tunnels they passed flicked by like sparks. The change in pressure made Peter's ears hurt, and he had to blow them clear as he'd been taught. The stop nearly two miles beneath the surface was just as abrupt as the start.

After a few weeks Peter scarcely noticed the discomfort of the cage. The mine work became routine. Every morning the work gang marched to the mine before the 5:30 whistle. On the way, it would pass the night shift trudging back to the barracks.

At the gate, the gang changed passbooks for mine passes, was searched, and walked to the cage. Then it was down the shaft and into the dark where ore was blasted and drilled from the gold vein. Warm, heavy air. Helmet lights on sweaty bodies and wet rock walls. Load ore into cars and push them down the tracks. Up the shaft for half an hour of lunch — porridge, hard bread, meat — and stretch out in the dirt. Down again until dusk. March to barracks with eyes red-rimmed from dust. Talk of home. Sleep on concrete to the rumble of dynamite below.

Peter had planned to save all his pay. On Saturdays, when most of the miners went off to dance in the beer halls of the black areas, he stayed in the barracks. There he could sleep, talk, and play the guitar, or find someone to write a letter for him to his wife.

Then, one Saturday afternoon, Peter and another Xhosa took a bus to downtown Johannesburg. The tense sensation that Peter had felt in Umtata bothered him even more in this vast white city. But the glittering shop windows filled with fancy clothes and gadgets fascinated him, and he wandered the streets for hours.

"Hey, look at these." Peter called his friend over to the window of a shoe store. "Look at that pair of black shoes. Nice, eh?"

"Not for mine boys."

"When I return to the kraal, I won't be a mine boy. Come on. I have the money." They entered the store and waited until a salesman came over and looked at them questioningly. Peter pointed to the shoes, and they were brought over. His friend, who spoke a little Afrikaans,* the language of South Africa's Dutch-descended Afrikaners, translated for him.

"They're nice, eh? I'll see if they fit."

"Natives are not allowed to try on shoes or clothes in this shop," the salesman said.

"But what if they don't fit?"

"The rule is..."

"I'll buy them anyway." Peter was angry. He thrust the money roughly at the man, grabbed the shoes, and turned toward the door.

215

"Now listen. If you people think you can..." The salesman didn't finish. Peter and his friend had gone.

Outside, Peter walked quickly, as if to get away from danger. Then he turned into a side street, sat down on the sidewalk curb, and took off his sandals.

"I'll try them on here," Peter said. He began to loosen the laces of one of the new shoes. He pushed his foot into it.

"Hey there. What are you doing?" The voice came from a white policeman standing behind them. "Move along. No. Wait. Let's see your passbooks." They pulled them out.

The policeman turned to the back page of Peter's book and read out his name.

"Zima, eh? Well, Zima, where'd you get those fancy shoes?" He grabbed the one Peter was holding.

"He bought them," Peter's friend explained.

"Fine. Let's see your receipt."

"He doesn't have a receipt," said the friend.

"All right, you two." The policeman made a grab for Peter's arm. Peter's friend began to run. Bewildered, Peter twisted away and ran too. With only one shoe, he couldn't make much speed, but the policeman didn't bother to chase them. In an hour, the two friends were back in the compound.

Peter was ashamed and angry at spending a week's pay on the shoes and then losing one. He should have grabbed it back. Why had he run, anyway? He'd done nothing wrong. The shoe salesman and the policeman had left him with a bitterness against the whites he hadn't felt before. In the Transkei he had had almost no contact with whites. At the mine, his white boss was tough but usually fair. Now he vowed never to return to downtown Johannesburg.

Peter told some of the other miners about the shoes. They only laughed at him.

216

"You were lucky to get away. They would have locked you up."

He found that many of them had spent weeks and sometimes months in the city jail. The police would arrest a man for not carrying a passbook. Or for quitting a job. Or for traveling to another city without a special permit. Some of the men had been picked up for selling beer in the native locations.

"All a white man cares about is your strong black back, Zima," one of the miners told him. "Keep quiet, stay put, do what you're told, and you'll keep out of trouble."

That night Peter remembered an old Xhosa story he had often heard around the fire in the kraal. It was about a young girl who went at dusk to the seashore to find a beautiful shell. A wicked spirit grabbed her and locked her up in a barrel. The spirit made the girl sing whenever he beat on the barrel.

One day the spirit unknowingly took the barrel to the kraal of the girl's family. When she sang, her mother and father recognized her voice. That night they drugged the spirit into a deep sleep and took their daughter out of the barrel. In her place, they put a nest of poisonous snakes. The next time the spirit beat on the barrel, the snakes came out and killed him.

"Some day," Peter said to himself, "some day when the white man beats on the black barrel, there will be no more singing."

Double-check

Review

1. What is a kraal?

2. What did cattle symbolize among the Xhosa people?

3. Why was Transkei called a homeland for women and children only?

4. Why did Peter carry a passbook?

5. What is "Afrikaans"?

Discussion

1. Peter tried to resist leaving the traditional life of the Xhosas, but he had to leave his village to earn money. Is this the future for *all* African villagers? Is traditional life doomed once a cash economy is introduced to a country? Will African cities continue to grow at the expense of villages and traditional ways of making a living? Give reasons to support your answers.

2. Why do you think Peter wanted to buy the shoes? Did he want them for his feet or as a symbol of his changing life? Do you think he would have bought them if he hadn't become angry in the store? Do you think most people would have reacted the way Peter did in the store? Explain your answers.

3. Do you think all white people in South Africa would act the way the shoe salesman did? Why do you think the policeman did not chase Peter and his friend? Do you think Peter will feel bitterness and hatred toward all white people now? Should he? Why, or why not?

Activities

1. South Africa is one of the world's leading producers of gold and diamonds. Some students might research and report on how these are mined, refined, and marketed throughout the world.

2. Two or more students might take turns role-playing a conversation between Peter and Mugendi or Moigai in which they talk about their decisions to leave their villages and their different experiences in the large cities they went to.

3. A committee of students might pretend to be travel agents for your class. They could solicit class opinions, and then plan a three-month trip to Africa for the class — listing cities and other areas the class would like to visit and the people the class would like to talk with.

Skills

SOUTHERN AFRICA

Use the map on page 211 to answer the following questions.

1. Which ocean lies to the east of South Africa?
(a) Mozambique   (b) Atlantic   (c) Indian

2. How many countries border Zimbabwe?
(a) none   (b) five   (c) four

Use the maps on pages 171 and 211 to answer the following questions.

3. Which European country controlled Namibia in 1914?
(a) Great Britain   (b) Portugal   (c) Germany

4. What is the present name of the former British colony of Nyasaland?
(a) Malawi   (b) Zimbabwe   (c) Zambia

5. Which foreign country in 1914 controlled the area that is now Peter Zima's "homeland"?
(a) Spain   (b) Great Britain   (c) Portugal

EPILOGUE

PUTTING
DOWN
NEW ROOTS

OUT ON THE PLAINS of Africa a mighty tree grows. It is known as the baobab.* Despite its massive size, the baobab never gets too far off the ground. Its sturdy, wrinkled trunk inches upward like so many slats in a barrel. Its sprawling branches reach outward, instead of upward, as if to protect the land which gives it life.

221

As guardian of its surroundings, the baobab is a very patient tree. By day it allows itself to be used as a scratching post by elephants and other beasts of the African plain. Once the sun goes down, the baobab becomes a home for the creatures of the night. Bats and owls hide among its branches, gazing out on a world that was old when recorded time began.

Experts guess that some baobabs have existed for 2,500 years. If so, the trees are among the oldest living things on earth. Rocked by the wind and teased by the rain, these great gray trees have held fast to the grassy earth. In the earth they have found a way to endure.

In some respects, the story of the baobab is the story of Africa itself. Like the branches of the "barrel tree," most Africans have sought to protect the land which gives them life.

To a herder or farmer, this is merely a matter of common sense. The land, after all, is a provider — a producer of food. But to most Africans, the land has a much deeper significance. It is a resting place for ancestors, a home for the living, and a promise of life for those yet unborn.

And so the land has been respected. It has been celebrated in song and story. It has been depicted in many dances and worshiped in many prayers. This is an attitude of sincere devotion. As South African novelist Alan Paton has written about the land: "Keep it, guard it, care for it, for it keeps men, guards men, cares for men. Destroy it and man is destroyed."

Now, for the first time, some Africans believe that this devotion is imperiled. They say it is in danger of being swallowed up in the tides of modern life. These people claim that too many highways now cover the land and too many giant dams abuse it. They fear that the land itself is about to be destroyed.

◆§ **New ways are taking hold.
Will the new prove
as durable as the old?**

*Today's African leaders are trying to strike
a balance between yesterday's customs and
tomorrow's needs. How does this young
African leader appear to be doing that while he
tackles problems faced by farmers of his region?*

Sometimes the fears are even broader. For not only the land is threatened. In the past half century, changes on the continent have been overwhelming. New cities have sprouted, new nations have been created, new schoolhouses have been built. Old ways of life based on a close relationship with the land have been tossed and buffeted by the winds of change. New ways are taking hold, but some wonder if the new will prove as durable as the old.

Will the future bring new dignity to the African family system? Will it provide a place for the customs and traditions of the village? Will it help Africans to protect the many things which they have made enduring? Or will it merely bring disruption, sweeping away all the remnants of the past?

There can be no final answers to these questions. Rather, the answers are up to Africans themselves. In the course of the present century, many of their roots have been upended. Now they are facing the challenge of putting down new roots without destroying those old ones which remain.

Pronunciation Guide

The following system translates each syllable into the nearest common English equivalent. Syllables set in capitals are accented. If the whole word is in lower-case letters, the stress on each syllable is approximately equal. Principal sound equivalents are:

a (as in cat)
ah (as in arm)
aw (as in soft)
ay (as in ale)
ch (as in chair)
ee (as in eat)
eh (as in end)
g (as in go)
igh (as in ice)
ih (as in ill)
j (as in joke)

k (as in keep)
oh (as in old)
oo (as in food)
o͝o (as in foot)
ow (as in out)
s (as in sit)
t (as in tin)
u (as in cube)
uh (unaccented a as in sofa)
ur (as in urn)
z (as in zone)

Accra — uh-KRAH
Afrikaans — ahf-rih-KAHNZ
Afrikaners — ahf-rih-KAH-nerz
Agni — ah-nee
Aka — AH-kuh
Allah — AL-uh
Amah — AH-muh
Amharic — am-HAIR-ihk
Angola — ang-GOH-luh
animism — AN-ih-mihz'm
apartheid — uh-PAHR-tayt
Ashanti — uh-SHAHN-tee
Askia Mohammed — as-KEE-uh moh-HAM-ud

Bambuti — bahm-BOO-tee
baobab — BOW-bab

Barbados — bahr-BAY-dohz
Boers — bohrz
boloki — bah-loh-kee
Bomboma — bahm-BOH-muh
Napoleon Bonaparte — nuh-POH-lee-un BOH-nuh-pahrt
Botswana — bah-TSWAH-nuh
Burundi — boo-ROON-dee

Cameroons — KAM-er-oonz

Dar es Salaam — DAHR ehs suh-LAHM

Equateur — ee-kwah-TUR
Olaudah Equiano — oh-LOW-duh ee-KAW-noh
Ethiopia — ee-thee-OH-pee-uh

Akwasi Gambaga — AHK-wee-zee gam-BAH-guh
Ghana — GAH-nuh
Ghanaians — gah-NAY-unz
Guinea — GIHN-ee

harmattan — hahr-muh-TAN
Hausa — HOU-suh

Ibo — EE-boh
Islam — IHS-lum
Ituri — ee-TOOR-ee

Johannesburg — joh-HAN-ihs-burg

Kalahari — kaw-lah-HAHR-ee
Kaminda — ka-MIHN-duh
Karenga — kahr-EHN-guh
Kassi — kuh-SEE
Kente — KEHN-tay
Kenya — KEHN-yuh
Jomo Kenyatta — JOH-moh ken-YAH-tuh
Khoisan — KOY-suhn
Kikuyu — kih-KOO-u
Kilimanjaro — kihl-ih-man-JAH-roh
Kinshasa — kihn-SHAH-suh
Kobina — koh-BEE-nuh
Koran — KOH-ruhn
Koumbi — koom-bee
kraals — krahlz

Kumasi — koo-MAH-see
kwashiorkor — kwah-she-ohr-kohr

lapa — LAH-pah
(Louis) Leakey — LEE-kee
Liberia — ligh-BEER-ee-uh
Limpopo — lihm-POH-poh
Lubumbashi — loo-boom-bah-shee
Lusaka — loo-SAH-kuh

Madagascar — mad-uh-GAS-ker
makuta — muh-koot-uh
Malgache — mahl-GAHSH
Mali — MAH-lee
mama na bana — MAH-mah nah BAH-nah
Mande — MAN-day
Mandingoes — man-DIHNG-gohz
manioc — MAN-ih-ok
mansa — MAHN-suh
Masai — muh-SIGH
Matadi — muh-TAH-dee
matrilineal — ma-trih-LIHN-ee-uhl
moambe — moo-ahm-be
Mohammed — moh-HAM-ud
Moigai — moo-ee-guy
Mombasa — mahm-BAH-suh
mongongo — mahn-gahn-goh
Mossi — MOH-sih
Mosu — moh-SEH
Mozambique — moh-zuhm-BEEK
Mugendi — moo-gen-dee
Muranga — moor-rahn-guh
Musa — moo-suh

Nairobi — nigh-ROH-bee
Namibia — nah-MIH-bee-uh
Natal — na-TAHL
Ndbele — en-deh-beh-leh
Ngai — n'guy
Niger-Congo — NIGH-jer KAHN-goh
Nigeria — nigh-JIHR-ee-uh
Nshombo — ehn-SHAHM-boh

okapi — oh-KAH-pee
Olduvai — OHL-duh-vay

Palos — PAH-lohs
plantain — PLAN-tihn
polygyny — pol-LIHJ-uh-nee
Pygmies — PIG-meez

Rhodesia — roh-DEE-zhuh
Rwanda — R'WAHN-duh

San — suhn
Senegal — sehn-ih-GAHL
Sindula — sihn-DOO-luh
Somali — soh-MAH-lee
Somalia — soh-MAH-lee-uh
Songhay — song-gay
Soninkes — son-in-kays
subsistence — suhb-SIHS-tehns
Sudanic — soo-DAN-ihk
Swahili — swah-HEE-lee

Tanganyika — tan-gan-YEE-kuh
Tanzania — tan-zuh-NEE-uh
Timbuktu — tihm-buk-TOO
Togoland — TOH-goh-land
Transkei — trans-KIGH

Uganda — u-GAN-duh
uhuru — oo-HOO-roo
Umtata — oŏm-TAH-tuh

Wanjiku — wahn-jee-koo

Xhosa — KAW-zuh

Yoruba — YOH-roŏ-buh

Zaïre — za-EAR
Zambezi — zam-BEE-zee
Zambia — ZAM-bee-uh
Zanzibar — ZAN-zih-bahr
(Peter) Zima — zee-muh
Zimbabwe — zihm-BAH-bwee
Zinj — zihn'j
Zinjanthropus — ZIHN-jan-thruh-puhs
Zulu — ZOO-loo

Index

*Photograph

231